P9-BEE-225

The Second Wind

For the Generation Following — The World Changers of the 21st Century

by Freda Lindsay

Published by
Christ For The Nations Inc.
P.O. Box 769000
Dallas, TX 75376-9000
Phone: (214) 376-1711
Web Site: http://www.cfni.org
E-Mail: info@cfni.org

Printed 1999
© Christ For The Nations Inc. 1999

All Scripture NKJV unless otherwise noted.

Dedication

To the friends of Christ For The Nations, young and old, that have prayed for and supported this worldwide missions' ministry — some from its very beginning 51 years ago, I dedicate this book. There were those who sacrificially, regularly sent to us a dollar or two a month. These were usually pensioners. White collar laborers could and did give more. A few, whom God had singularly prospered financially, gave abundantly — without whom, we wouldn't have survived. Then on occasion, our ministry was named in a will or trust. Funds from these came at times when we had a great need, either at our Dallas base or on one of our many overseas projects. These involved one of our 40 foreign Bible schools, or one of our 10,314 Native Churches that we've helped build.

When notice of the decease of one of our partners reaches us, it always grieves our hearts. We're deeply moved and appreciative when one of those friends named us in their will.

My gratitude also goes to my great niece, Patti Conn, managing editor of Christ For The Nations, and to Naomi Westbrook, my personal secretary. Without their dedicated assistance, this book would not have been published.

So to all of you dear ones, we send our love and appreciation for caring and sharing. Together, we shall stand before our great God when He passes out the rewards, and together we'll be recompensed by the fruits of this ministry. Thank you and blessings!

Table of Contents

Part IV: World Changers Network

Part V: A Family of World Changers

Part VI: Wisdom for World Changers

Introduction

Every responsible person will give serious thought to how his personal assets will be divided when he or she leaves this world. But of far greater importance is: What do we leave in the spiritual realm for our successors? Do we have any obligation?

The truth is: We do. In fact, what we leave to the next generation in the spiritual realm, is far more important than what we bequeath in the natural. We need to tell that "which we have heard and known, and our fathers have told us. We will not hide *them* from their children, telling to the generation to come the praises of the LORD, and His strength and His wonderful works that He has done" (Psa. 78:3,4).

David added, "I will sing of the mercies of the LORD forever; with my mouth will I make known Your faithfulness to all generations" (Psa. 89:1). That's where our obligation ceases: when we have reached all generations!

It has been said that no one is a success until first he has trained his successor. And that is exactly what Christ For The Nations has been doing for the last 51 years — training leaders — world shakers, world changers.

In this my sixth book, I have begun first by introducing to you from the Bible, men and women leaders God used to change history. Their qualifications at times seemed very few. Some of their backgrounds, in the natural, would appear to make them unfit for the great tasks ahead — until God came on the scene and supplied what was lacking.

Next, I listed several key men with whom we joined our efforts. The results have been phenomenal.

Following, the thrilling accounts of some of our 26,000+ Christ For The Nations Institute alumni, as they labor around the world, will set your soul afire.

I've included then the remarkable stories of how God has called and is using my own three children — with extremely different makeups — in very diversified fields, all of them working full time for the Lord.

Then, in conclusion, I add a manual of "how-to's" for the next generation — the ones who will cross the finish line. Some are already in the race. Others are even now gearing up. And, as when God sent the Holy Spirit like a mighty rushing wind (Acts 2:1-4), to prepare that generation for a revival, so today, He is again calling and anointing this generation, as they get their second wind, to bring closure. Closure to what? To the fulfillment of God's plan to rescue a world in which fallen man has proven himself incapable of solving his own problems, and where God will take charge.

Part I: World Changers in Training

Chapter One

Training Winners

L ife is not a sprint. Life is a marathon — a cross-country, disciplined commitment to win in the eternal Olympics.

I recall hearing Jackie Joyner-Kersee speak at a women's conference. She was acclaimed the world's finest woman athlete, having received an outstanding number of gold, silver and bronze Olympic medals.

She told of the extensive, often excruciating pain she endured in her body while training for "the big one" — how at times at the finish line, she would fall down with her mouth full of blood because of the effort she had exerted in her dedication to be a winner.

Kersee's definition of how she had accomplished her goals was: "desire, discipline and dedication. Omit any of these qualities and one's likelihood of being a winner is usually nil."

Competitors in races don't usually "give it their very best" until right near the end — after they get their second wind. Then they "go for the gold," utilizing every ounce of strength they can muster as they strain toward the finish line. In a relay race, the fastest runner is always the last one on the team to carry the baton.

A "how to be a winner" maxim says this:

> Do you not know that those who run in a race all
> run, but one receives the prize? Run in such a way
> that you may obtain *it*. And everyone who com-
> petes for *the prize* is temperate in all things. Now
> **they** *do it* to obtain a perishable crown, but **we** *for*
> an imperishable *crown*. Therefore I run thus: not
> with uncertainty. Thus I fight: not as *one who* beats
> the air. But I discipline my body and bring *it* into
> subjection (I Cor. 9:24-27).

One must know the value of the prize and be willing to
pay the price. One must also be aware of certain roadblocks,
such as overconfidence, misguided zeal, lack of training,
being unprepared mentally and spiritually, or ignorance of
one's competitor's abilities. As General Douglas MacArthur
said, "The better one knows his enemy's capabilities, the
better he knows how to fight him."

The world sits full of healthy, talented, sometimes highly-
educated individuals who dream of someday being a winner.
They occupy the grandstands, often applauding their heroes, but
have zero dedication for any needful discipline to succeed.

As I write this book, Christ For The Nations is celebrating
our 51st year of ministry around the world. In those 51 years,
we have helped build 10,314 Native Churches; we have
produced millions of Christian books and sent most of them
to developing nations free of charge; we have helped support
several orphanages; we have sent disaster relief to Third-
World nations.

In 1970, my husband Gordon and I started Christ For The
Nations Institute in Dallas, Texas. Since that time, more than

26,000 students have been trained. Now our alumni are spread across the globe. Combining their unique, God-given abilities with the training they received at CFNI for Christian life and ministry, some are building the Kingdom via the marketplace and some through full-time ministry. And today, we have 40 associate Bible schools in 26 countries, and the number is growing.

As you can see, CFN's ministry has touched virtually every country of the world. Are we finished running our race? No, we are just getting our "second wind." Another generation of leaders is strategizing and mobilizing for the 21st century. They plan to continue our effective missions endeavors. And they purpose to train more world changers than ever before — men and women with the same attributes Kersee has: desire, discipline and dedication. The race we are running has eternal significance, and we are determined to win!

That desire, discipline and dedication must of necessity reside in the heart and goal of every achiever — whether believer or non-believer. And God is not limited by one's past, lack of talents or education.

Take my brother, Fred, the oldest son of my parents' 12 children. He attended a one-room country school in Canada, while at the same time helping my dad farm. In 1919 when he was age 16, we moved to Oregon City, Oregon, to another farm. The younger members of the family attended a one-room country school, but Fred was now "too big" to enroll. So his formal education came to an end, though he probably had not even finished the eighth grade.

But Fred had fortunately learned to read and had a great appetite for knowledge, especially in the mechanical arena.

Plus amazingly, he developed a love and appreciation for classical music like that of the world-renowned violinist, Fritz Kreisler.

Fred was fortunate enough to secure a *Popular Mechanics* manual of the day, and devoured it. Soon he was tinkering with motorcycles. Then came an appetite for cars. He would literally "concoct" all sorts of weird combinations using body parts from different cars to create underslung vehicles, which attracted the curiosity and fancy of the men and boys of our neighborhood.

Then came Fred's fascination for airplanes. That was in 1926 when no one had heard of commercial flights! But Fred decided he would build himself a plane. So he set up shop in our small, one-car garage — pounding away often into the wee hours of the morning — usually with several teenagers looking on.

One night, my mother's little foot-pedaled Singer sewing machine disappeared. She found it in the garage! Fred had appropriated it to sew his wings!

The next thing our family saw was that one side and the back of the garage walls were being torn down! "What now?" my dad asked. Fred's reply was that he "figured out" the wings he was making were too small to lift the plane, so he had to enlarge and make new ones. So for about two years, the pounding in the garage continued through many late hours.

Then the exciting, long-awaited news was heralded: The plane was finished and ready to fly! Our entire family stood on our porch, along with neighborhood men and boys, as Fred pulled his one-seater monoplane from its garage moorings. With one of his underslung concoctions, he pulled the plane over the unpaved street toward the Vancouver, Washington, tiny landing strip — one of the first "airports" in the area. The wings he had to carry separately.

I recall my old grandfather, who had never believed Fred could build a plane, standing on our porch watching and crying aloud, "He'll go up in the sky, come down in a crash, and kill himself." Mother thought he should fly low and slow.

Soon Fred was flying all over the area, to the delight of all of us. He kept the plane for about a year, then sold it, I believe, for about $450 — a lot of money in those days!

How did Fred accomplish this feat? It was his desire, dedication, discipline and determination that carried the day. Fortunately, Fred had a strong love for God, and blessed many a family by repairing their cars — often "for free."

And now, as I write this book, an amazing thing is transpiring: It seems the Lord is permitting the field to be cleared, to make room for the second string. Several giants in key positions in the ministry have gone to their eternal reward, including John Osteen, Jim Zirkle, Costa Deir, Benson Idahosa, Marfa Cabrera, Winston Nunes and earlier, Lester Sumrall, Daisy Osborn, plus several more, including some who are presently battling for their lives.

That next generation that has been in training, waiting and watching on the sideline benches, is now eager to be thrown into the battle, to win and to carry the day. This new generation could well be the one that will achieve the goal to witness God's Kingdom being established on the earth. Let's not fail to pray for them, support them, and at times when God leads, encourage them with a word of wisdom. Doing this, I believe, will please God.

Chapter Two

What Are We Passing On?

Gordon used to say, "God gives a nation the kind of leader it deserves."

Man was not created to live for himself. It was the Creator Who inspired the psalmist to write, "Tell *it* to the generation following" (Psa. 48:13). We have not fulfilled God's purpose for our lives until we have so exemplified Jesus that the hearts of our families turn to Him. But our obligation does not end there. There is a whole world full of "our generation," many of whom were reared by godless parents, who in turn were subject to the same lack of spiritual training.

As we reflect on the end of this millennium and the coming of the next, we see a world steeped in corruption and unable to solve its own problems. A death-producing agenda lies before us. The best way to understand the present and prepare for the future is to turn to the Scriptures.

Samuel, a prophet of God, judged Israel all the days of his life. Though a mighty man of God, Samuel somehow failed to influence his own sons for the Lord. The Bible says, "His sons did not walk in his ways; they turned aside after dishonest gain, took bribes, and perverted justice" (I Sam. 8:3). PKs (preachers kids) gone bad! (As my late husband, Gordon, used to say, "Few preachers can handle prosperity, popularity and power.") Samuel commendably kept others' vineyards, but foolishly neglected his own. He failed in the most important calling of all — his ministry to his children.

So disillusioned Israel cried out, "Give us a king" (I Sam. 8:6). God relented to their demands and gave them Saul — a tall, handsome, young man. But first, He warned them that this king would be a dictator who would use Israel's sons and daughters and all they owned to ingratiate himself as a world ruler. God gave them the man they deserved. In the end, Saul brought great judgment on his nation.

God plainly gives requirements for leaders: "A bishop then must be ... one who rules his own house well, having *his* children in submission with all reverence (for if a man does not know how to rule his own house, how will he take care of the church of God?)" (I Tim. 3:2,4,5).

God is giving America the kind of president it deserves — one who is as wicked and perverse as his constituents. There is no doubt great judgment coming on this nation — short of a mighty revival of repentance and a turning away from its gross sins.

Writes Leslie K. Hedger in her book, *The Parched Soul of America: Using the Law to Guarantee Libertarianism*:

- Promiscuity is promoted in schools.
- Sodomy is politically protected.
- Pornography is distributed to criminals.
- Economic reforms attack the family.
- Baby killing is made a privacy issue.

- The UN becomes our military commander

... a house condemned for structural damage.

We are without hope but for God! Man is destroying himself. Nations are committing genocide!

Today books are being written and films and videos are being produced and distributed about men who were once thought to be great world leaders. Now they are being exposed as evil, corrupt leaders, and the United States' leaders are at the top of the list.

The Bible has long stated, "Be sure your sin will find you out" (Num. 32:23). Note it does not say that God will find you out nor that the Holy Spirit will find you out — or even that Jesus will find you out! It plainly reveals what will expose you. It is your very own sin that will hound you! Hound you to your dying day, unless you repent of your sin. Even then, the memory of it may linger until the day of your death!

It's not only unbelievers who are being exposed, until it seems there's not a political leader to be found who does not have a sinful past, but even worse, many of our supposedly spiritual leaders in the Church are being confronted and confessing to unsavory pasts.

An ad in *U.S.A. Today* (11/02/98) summarizes well America's decaying spiritual and moral state:

Dear Nation:

We know that the president lies!

And we don't care!

We know he committed perjury to the Grand Jury!

And we don't care!

We know the president has been repeatedly

unfaithful to his wife.

And we don't care!

We know our children want to be like him!

And we don't care!

Because the economy is great and he says he is the reason why and *we know we can always believe him!*

Morality and integrity do not matter!

Everyone knows that! We have more important things to worry about!

Yours truly,

The American people

Paid for by Tesamen Enterprises Inc. — People Who Do Care

Chapter Three

The Road Ahead —
Where Does It Lead?

G ordon used to say to our children, "Learn by the mis-
takes of others, because you won't live long enough to
make them all yourself."

How fortunate is the person who comes from a godly
family, a godly heritage. At times when we've prayed for
engaged couples at Christ For The Nations Institute the last
week of each semester, I remind them of this: "Some of you
don't realize you are not just marrying your fiance(e). The
truth of the matter is, you are marrying his or her whole
family."

There are generational curses that can harass a couple.
These consequences of sin can and must be dealt with.
Victory over the grip of ungodly past generations comes
through concentrated fasting and prayer until that curse is
broken. Many couples know little or nothing about this,
"visiting the iniquity of the fathers upon the children to the
third and fourth *generations* of those who hate Me" (Ex.
20:5). Thus they spend their lives battling addictions and
compulsions, the source of which they don't comprehend. If

these curses are not dealt with, they have to wonder about their effect on their offspring.

God has made Himself very plain so that no one need be in ignorance. In Deuteronomy 27 and 28, He spells out exactly what will bring blessing to man and what will bring a curse.

Hear what God says to those who love and obey Him:

> Therefore know that the LORD your God, He *is* God, the faithful God who keeps covenant and mercy for a thousand generations with those who love Him and keep His commandments (Deut. 7:9).

To those who turn from their sins, God says,

> "My Spirit who *is* upon you, and My words which I have put in your mouth, shall not depart from your mouth, nor from the mouth of your descendants, nor from the mouth of your descendants' descendants," says the LORD, "from this time forevermore" (Isa. 59:21).

The fruit of a curse or blessing is seldom limited to the individual who incurred it. It usually affects the family, and sometimes, the community, the city and the nation. The curse can be broken when a person is genuinely born again. Or it can continue and bring a series of tragedies.

The book, *The Tale of Two Men,* is a graphic example of this truth. It traces the descendants of two men living in New England in the same time period: The first was Jonathan Edwards, the mighty preacher who lived from 1703-1758. Through him, a mighty revival came to America, especially along the Eastern seaboard. The second was Max Jux, an indolent, a lazy sluggard.

Jonathan Edwards broke the family curse, and out of his genealogy has come one vice president, 65 college professors, 13 college presidents, three senators, 30 judges, 100 lawyers, 60 doctors, and 100 preachers and missionaries.

However, Max Jux did not break the curse. Out of his genealogy has come 310 bums, 150 criminals including seven murderers, 100 alcoholics, and 200 prostitutes.

> He who believes in the Son has everlasting life;
> and he who does not believe the Son shall not see
> life, but the wrath of God abides on him (Jn. 3:36)

> Life is a coin. You can spend it any way you wish,
> but you can spend it only once (Lillian Dickin).

God did not leave His creation to wander aimlessly on an uncharted course. From the beginning of time, He placed in the heart of every human the instinct, the knowledge that there is a God ... the great I Am (Rom 1:20)!

In the end time, He promised, "And it shall come to pass afterward (after man's allotted time is running out) that I will pour out (great abundance) My Spirit on all flesh (every class). ... Whoever calls on the name of the LORD shall be saved" (Joel 2:28,32).

Prophecy at times has a double fulfillment like the Scripture above, which no doubt referred not only to the outpouring of the Holy Spirit on the Day of Pentecost (Acts 2:4), but also to the revival taking place in our day.

> And it shall come to pass afterward that I will pour
> out My Spirit on all flesh; your sons and your
> daughters shall prophesy, your old men shall
> dream dreams, your young men shall see visions.

... And it shall come to pass that whoever calls on the name of the LORD shall be saved. For in Mount Zion and in Jerusalem there shall be deliverance. As the LORD has said, among the remnant whom the LORD calls (Joel 2:28,32).

However, at the same time that this mighty outpouring takes place, God warns that in the last days, "Evil men ... will grow worse and worse" (II Tim. 3:13). Despite the increasing knowledge in virtually every area of life, man is not getting better. In so many areas, society is not improving, but deteriorating.

Thank God, we have a choice: the Lord's way of living for our Maker or the self-deceived path that leads to destruction. Each of us must make that choice. God said, "I call heaven and earth as witnesses today against you, *that* I have set before you life and death, blessing and cursing; therefore choose life, that both you and your descendants may live" (Deut. 30:19).

Chapter Four

Opportunities in Abundance!

G ordon used to say, "Find out where God is moving and move with Him."

Amazingly, 70 percent of the growth of the Church has been in this century; most of it, in the last five years.

God said to the prophet Daniel, "Shut up the words, and seal the book until the time of the end; many shall run to and fro, and knowledge shall increase" (Dan. 12:4).

Today we see the increase of knowledge as never before in history — doubling every nine months in some areas. Unfortunately, wisdom has been left far behind.

But what opportunities the new technology affords us! During Hurricane Mitch in November 1998, when devastating winds and mudslides knocked out electricity and telephones, we were desperate to secure news from our graduates and missionaries stationed in Honduras. We called missionary Peter Jurka in Tegucigalpa, who owned a cellular phone. Within a couple of minutes, Peter was giving us a firsthand report of exactly what the situation was. (Even the young people — by the millions — carry cellular phones.)

Now with modern technology, machines have become appliances. More computers were purchased in the U.S. last year than TVs. Cyberspace is offering us worlds to explore. With e-mail and faxes, I can communicate in minutes with my daughter and her family who live and minister in Israel. Years ago, I hesitated to telephone her even once a month because of the cost. My letters took weeks to reach her.

Just yesterday, my eldest son showed me a small computer (about the size of a lady's purse) he had purchased. It carries all the addresses of his several hundred customers for whom he prints. On it he receives his faxes almost instantly from his printing plant in Belarussia, where he prints millions of Bibles, New Testaments and gospel books. No matter where he travels worldwide, his office is in constant touch with him.

Plus radio, television, Christian films and videos are reaching multitudes with the Gospel. The *Jesus* film, produced by Dr. Bill Bright of Campus Crusade and translated into 484 languages, has been seen by 1.6 billion.

Science now envisions anti-Alzheimer's microchips in the brain; lunar resorts; chip-enhanced brains to end aging; and paper-clip-size machines with genius far beyond that of Einstein and Mozart combined, according to *U.S. News & World Report* (12/18/98). Predictions are that computer chips will soon be cheaper than "bubble gum wrappers," and will be imbedded in everything from tie clasps to lane markers on streets.

"Computers will have amassed all the world's accumulated knowledge, and have read all the world's works," says Roy Kurzweil, who accurately forecasted the emergence of the Web over a decade ago. Smart machines' development is in the process of being further advanced. New species of high-yield food plants will help feed the world's starving. The search continues for the fountain of youth. It is now possible that cures for cancer, diabetes, heart disease and other prolific killers will be attained.

Cloning of humans is attracting the research of scientists worldwide. The likelihood of neural implanting and genetic alterations to enable one to learn to play the violin in an hour or to speak dozens of languages stagger the mind. With the population reaching ten billion in 50 years, underground dwellings could become common. On the other hand, global warming could produce massive floods. Or one vicious virus could clean the planet of human life. Who can tell what lies ahead? Believers must keep God-directed. Psalm 16:11 promises: "You will show me the path of life; in Your presence *is* fullness of joy; at Your right hand *are* pleasures forevermore."

In spite of all this amazing technology, what is a more awesome miracle than human life? Says licensed psychologist, Richard Dobbins, Ph. D., "Just stop and think: Approximately nine months after a father's sperm and a mother's ovum unite, a baby is born with eyes that see in three dimensions, ears that hear in stereo, and a digestive chemical laboratory that can transform liquids into skin, muscle, nerve tissue, bone, blood and hair. One simply cannot grasp the wonder of it all." How true!

Part II:
World
Changers
From Bible
Times

Chapter Five

God Handpicks Leaders — First There Was Abraham

God created man in the Garden of Eden, but man "blew it." Then instead of serving the Creator, people made themselves gods of wood, stone, or clay, or worshiped the stars, moon, trees, animals — or whatever!

There came the time when God decided to choose a leader, a progenitor of the race that would serve Him with all his heart. This was to be a chosen people (Psa. 33:12), a "special treasure" (Psa. 135:4), "the apple of His eye" (Deut. 32:10), "a kingdom of priests and a holy nation" (Ex. 19:6), "a name of joy, a praise, and an honor before all nations of the earth" (Jer. 33:9). This nation was to be called Israel!

Whom would God choose to be Israel's leader? Surely it would need to be someone very special. Right? God looked over the whole earth and selected a man, Abram, later called Abraham. He found him in Ur of the Chaldees (modern day Iraq) in a family of idol worshipers (Josh. 24:2).

God spoke to Abraham saying, "Get out of your country,

from your family (Abraham took with him his nephew, Lot, who later caused him countless troubles) ... to a land that I will show you. I will make you a great nation; I will bless you and make your name great; and you shall be a blessing. I will bless those who bless you, and I will curse him who curses you; and in you all the families of the earth shall be blessed" (Gen. 12:1-3). Later, God made a covenant with Abraham, saying, "To your descendants I have given this land, from the river of Egypt (the El Wadi) to the great river, the River Euphrates" (Gen. 15:18). Some 250 times, God promised specific land areas to the Jews.

So Abraham and his wife (they were childless at the time) left with Lot to travel 1,500 miles to a place ... somewhere. And Abraham, was no young man. By now, he was already 75 years old. But God led him step by step through dry deserts, mountains and rocky land. A few times he missed it: once by following his wife's advice to have a child with her maid, whose descendants have caused Israel grief to this day; and again twice when he pretended his wife was his sister, because he feared the leaders in the lands where he traveled would desire his beautiful wife, and would kill him to have her (Gen. 12:11-13; 20:2-11).

But God gave Abraham specific guidelines on which to build his life. Three times the Bible says Abraham was a friend of God and that "he believed in the LORD, and He accounted it to him for righteousness" (Gen. 15:6).

When Lot and his family were captured by four heathen kings, Abraham took 318 of his trained servants and rescued them (Gen. 14:12-16); Abraham was so grateful to God for the success, he paid tithes to the priest (ver. 20).

Earlier, God mightily prospered both Abraham and Lot with many cattle, so they decided to separate to allow more grazing land for the flocks. Abraham, generous example that he was, told Lot, "If *you take* the left, then I will go to the right; or, if *you go* to the right, then I will go to the left" (Gen. 13:9) — he could have first choice. Carnal "Lot chose for himself all the plain of Jordan" (ver. 11). He "saw all the plain of Jordan, that it *was* well watered everywhere" (ver. 10). The move for Lot brought him to Sodom and Gomorrah, where he eventually lost everything, including his wife.

But not so Abraham. God gave him and Sarah a miracle baby — Isaac, the progenitor of Jesus the Messiah, "for in Isaac your seed shall be called" (Gen. 21:12). Abraham wisely made possible the right choice of a godly woman, Rebekah, for Isaac's wife. God prospered Abraham and his seed exactly as He promised. Hebrews 11:8,9 says of Abraham, "By faith Abraham ... dwelt in the land of promise ... in tents with Isaac and Jacob, the heirs with him of the same promise." Yes, Abraham set the example and passed on his legacy of faith to the "generation(s) following," but also to us who are his seed, being children of faith (Gal. 3:6-9).

Chapter Six

A Role-Model Young Man

Few young men in the Bible, or even in the world, had the unstained, unblemished reputation Joseph had — especially when he suffered so much to maintain that distinction. The reason no doubt for his overcoming life was his unshakable trust in God. That faith put iron in his soul. Joseph, who was a man of determination, also showed his godly character through his great love and compassion.

Joseph was the son of Jacob and Rachel, his beloved wife. He was one of 12 sons, 10 of whom were half brothers. The favorite of his father, Joseph soon became hated by them. When Joseph was 17, he tended his father's flock with his half brothers. He saw some of the bad things they were doing, and reported to his father.

To make bad matters worse, Jacob had a beautiful coat of many colors designed for Joseph, which showed his special love for him. To top it all off, Joseph, before his entire family, told of two dreams he had. The second one was that the sun, moon and 11 stars would bow down to him. The apparent interpretation enraged his 10 brothers, and they hated him more than ever. Even his father rebuked him, but he kept wondering about Joseph's dreams.

Soon after his brothers left their fields in the valley of Hebron to find grazing land for the flock, Jacob sent Joseph to check on his brothers. So Joseph willingly went to see how they were doing. By this time, his brothers' jealousy and hatred for him had reached such a level that "when they saw him afar off, even before he came near them, they conspired against him to kill him" (Gen. 37:18). But Reuben, the eldest, came to Joseph's rescue. He said, "Let us not kill him. ... But cast him into this pit" (Gen. 37:21,22). Reuben planned to rescue Joseph later.

First, the brothers stripped him of his colorful coat. They then threw Joseph in a nearby pit, and coldheartedly, they sat down to eat a meal — probably one that Joseph had brought them from home. Later the brothers admitted, "we saw the anguish of his soul when he pleaded with us, and we would not hear" (Gen. 42:21).

But while Joseph was weeping in the pit and begging his brothers for mercy, a company of Ishmaelite traders on their way to Egypt traveled by. On their camels were spices, balm and myrrh from Gilead. Judah came up with an idea, "What profit *is there* if we kill our brother and conceal his blood? Come and let us sell him to the Ishmaelites ... and his brothers listened" (Gen. 37:26,27).

They followed Judah's advice, much to the consternation of Reuben when he returned (he apparently had left them for a short time). Being the eldest, he felt responsible for Joseph. But by now, the traders were long gone with their prize. So the brothers decided to kill a lamb, put its blood on Joseph's beautiful coat, and take it back to their father. They let him think that a wild beast had devoured him. Jacob mourned deeply for Joseph, and no one could comfort him.

Arriving in Egypt, the young Joseph was quickly sold to Potiphar, an officer of Pharaoh, and captain of the palace guard (ver. 36). It didn't take Potiphar long to recognize the sterling, pure character of his slave, Joseph. "His master saw that the LORD *was* with him and that the LORD made all he did to prosper in his hand. So Joseph found favor in his sight, and served him. Then he made him overseer of his house, and all *that* he had he put under his authority" (Gen. 39:3,4).

But Potiphar's wife also took note of this handsome Jewish young man in her household, and soon began to lust after him. Day after day, she no doubt made herself attractive with beautiful clothes, jewelry, perfumes and cosmetics. She probably made flirtatious and seductive gestures. But all to no avail. Joseph resisted her advances. Finally, when she boldly asked Joseph to sleep with her, he told her plainly, "How ... can I do this great wickedness, and sin against God?" (Gen. 39:9). His godly conviction held him steady!

This, however, did not turn this lustful woman, "as she spoke to Joseph day by day" from her evil obsession (ver. 10). One day, "when Joseph went into the house to do his work and none of the men of the house *was* inside, that she caught him by his garment, saying, 'Lie with me.' But he left his garment in her hand, and fled and ran outside" (ver. 11,12). The right way to handle temptation!

However, as soon as the other workers entered the house, she called to the men, claiming Joseph had tried to rape her, holding up his garment as "proof." When her husband returned home, she told him the same lie. Potiphar apparently believed her. Furious, he had Joseph thrown in prison.

"But the LORD was with Joseph and showed him mercy, and He gave him favor in the sight of the keeper of the prison. And the keeper of the prison committed to Joseph's hand all the prisoners who *were* in the prison; whatever they did there, it was his doing" (ver. 21,22). No, Joseph did not lose his faith in God.

One day, two prisoners — the king's cupbearer and baker — both had dreams, which they related to Joseph when he asked why they looked worried. God helped Joseph interpret the dreams: The baker would die at Pharaoh's next celebration, and the cupbearer would be restored to his former position. As the three said their shaloms (goodbyes), Joseph asked the butler to remember him to the king when he was restored. Joseph's interpretations were correct. But "two full years" passed, and the cupbearer, though restored to his position, apparently forgot all about Joseph.

Then Pharaoh had two dreams, but no one was able to interpret them. Now, the cupbearer remembered Joseph and told the king about his correct interpretation of his own dream and that of the baker. Joseph had been in prison 13 long years! He was now 30 years old.

So Joseph was pulled out of his dungeon (Gen. 41:14) dressed up, shaved,and made to look his best before Pharaoh. When Pharaoh told Joseph he needed an interpretation to his two dreams, Joseph responded, "*It is* not in me; God will give Pharaoh an answer of peace" (ver. 16). He listened to the dreams, and then God gave him the correct interpretation: There would be seven years of plenty, then seven years of famine. Then Joseph suggested a plan as to how Pharaoh should proceed: During the seven years of plenty, officials should collect one-fifth of the crops and store them for the seven years of famine.

The king and his advisers were so impressed, Joseph was immediately promoted to be the director of this project: "You shall be over my house, and all my people shall be ruled according to your word; only in regard to the throne will I be greater than you" (ver. 40). Pharaoh gave Joseph his own signet ring, clothed him in garments of fine linen, put a gold chain around his neck, and he rode in the chariot designated for the second in command.

The seven years of plenty came just as Joseph said they would. He carefully oversaw the collection and storage of food. There was so much food, they couldn't keep track of it all.

Then the seven years of terrible famine started. Soon the surrounding nations also became destitute. Their representatives headed for Egypt, where Joseph had laid up enormous food supplies from the seven years of plenty, as God had instructed him to do.

Even Israel was now experiencing famine. When Jacob heard of Egypt's plenty, he sent his 10 sons to buy food. He kept young Benjamin, Joseph's only real brother, with him in Hebron.

When the 10 half brothers appeared before Joseph, he immediately recognized them, but he did not identify himself. He inquired about their father and their other brother; he even accused them of being spies, which they vigorously denied. He then gave them an option: one of the brothers would be held in prison in Egypt while they returned to Hebron to get their youngest brother. The nine had little choice, so they bought food supplies and journeyed back to Israel. Joseph had requested their money be secretly restored to them by placing it in their filled sacks. When they discovered the money, they were terrified. "What *is* this *that* God has done to us?" (ver. 28).

When the nine told their father everything that had happened in Egypt, Jacob was very upset. First Joseph had been taken from him; now Simeon was imprisoned in Egypt; and they wanted to take Benjamin, his youngest.

After an interval, the food supply ran out, and Jacob directed his sons to return to Egypt to buy more. The nine refused to go unless they could take along Benjamin, as Joseph had stipulated. But Jacob wept, saying that his one son (Joseph), born of his beloved wife, Rachel, had been killed by a wild animal, and if they took Benjamin, the only other son born of her, he too would go to his grave from sorrow. The nine refused to return to Egypt, fearing Joseph would put them all in prison as spies — and also because of the money each had found in his sack of food.

Eventually, Jacob realized hunger would overtake all his family unless he allowed his sons to take Benjamin with them. The 10 made their way back to Egypt with gifts of honey, nuts, gum, myrrh and balm for Joseph.

Once again, Joseph recognized his brothers, but they still didn't recognize him. He had them taken to his house for dinner. They were terrified. When Joseph was introduced to Benjamin, he said, "God be gracious to you, my son" (Gen. 43:29). Joseph's heart was deeply moved at the sight of his younger brother, and he had to hurry away to his room, where he could weep unashamedly.

Joseph tested his brothers several more times. Finally to the amazement of his brothers, Joseph revealed his true identity. He was weeping so loudly, the Egyptians he had sent outside could hear him, as well as the house of Pharaoh. "'I *am* Joseph; does my father still live?' But his brothers could not answer him, for they were dismayed in his presence. And Joseph said to his brothers, 'Please come near to me.' So they came near. Then he said, 'I *am* Joseph your brother, whom you sold into Egypt. But now, do not therefore be grieved or angry with yourselves because you sold me here; for God sent me before you to preserve life. ... Hurry and go up to my father, and say to him ... 'God has made me lord of all Egypt; come down to me; do not tarry'" (Gen. 45:3-5,9). Joseph embraced all of his brothers, and they wept on each other's shoulders. He sent them back to Israel with wagons, supplies and donkeys.

The 11 sons now returned to tell their father Jacob about Joseph. "And Jacob's heart stood still, because he did not believe them. ... When he saw the carts which Joseph had sent to carry him, the spirit of Jacob ... revived. Then Israel said ... 'I will go and see him before I die'" (ver. 26-28). Jacob did go to Egypt, and when Joseph saw him, he "fell on his neck and wept on his neck a good while" (Gen. 46:29). With the blessing of Pharaoh, Joseph gave his father (who lived another 17 years in Egypt) and his brothers the best of the land. All of them had prostrated themselves before him, as Joseph, when a young lad, had seen in his dream.

Some have wondered why this virtuous youth, Joseph,

had to go through such pain and trials? He was hated, tempted, sold, falsely accused and imprisoned for 13 years — a mighty long time, especially for an innocent man!

These I believe are some of the reasons: 1) Joseph was his dad's favorite son, obviously pampered a bit, and he needed to learn submission to authority. 2) Since he was destined to be the second ruler in Egypt, he needed the discipline to master the Egyptian language, speaking without any accent. 3) Knowing about the Egyptian culture and religion was imperative. 4) His faith in God and His promises needed to be developed. 5) Forgiveness and mercy were qualities that he must practice to save his own family. 6) Humility was a needful qualification for anyone being promoted from a shepherd boy to a prime minister.

The truth is, we often learn more in the darkness than we do in the light — in times of failure or adversity more than in times of success or prosperity. Even in our dark moments, we're walking toward the light, and we can share in the light what we learned in darkness. We not only need to know what God is made of, but what we are made of, so we can strengthen the weak links of our lives.

Joseph, by learning these lessons, saved his family — father, brothers and millions more from starvation. He's an extraordinary role model for young people — and for everyone else too!

Chapter Seven

Then Came Moses

A few generations later, God had another "problem." He needed someone to lead a race of several million people who had been slaves in Egypt for 400 years, to the land that had been promised to them for centuries — since Abraham's day. Where could He find such a leader?

Again, He looked over the earth, and this time saw a beautiful crying baby boy in an ark of bulrushes hidden in the reeds of the Nile River of Egypt. He was Moses, the son of a Levite priest and his wife. He had been placed there by his mother, because an edict by King Pharaoh demanded all Jewish boys be killed; the Jewish population was growing too fast, he feared.

But that very morning, God laid it on the heart of Pharaoh's daughter to go with her maidens to bathe in the river at the exact spot where the ark had been placed. The crying baby, Moses, caught her attention, so she decided to take him to the palace to live with her. Moses' older sister, standing guard nearby, asked the princess, "Shall I go and call a nurse for you from the Hebrew women, that she may nurse the child for you?" (Ex. 2:7). The princess replied, "Go" (ver. 8). And his sister called their mother.

So Moses grew up in the palace amidst luxury, splendor and all the educational advantages afforded to royalty. But his Jewish mother, who nursed him, likely until age 4 or 5 as was their custom, apparently used every moment of opportunity to let him know of his Jewish heritage under God, even though he was now the princess' son.

One day when Moses was grown, the Bible says, "he went out to his brethren (the slaves) and looked at their burdens. And he saw an Egyptian beating a Hebrew, one of his brethren" (Ex. 2:11). Moses took it upon himself to kill the Egyptian, but later, when his act became known, fearing Pharaoh for his life, he fled to the desert and sat down by a well. There he met seven daughters of the priest of Midian, whose flocks he then helped water. They in turn, thinking he was an Egyptian shepherd, invited him home to meet their father, who later gave Moses one of his daughters, Zipporah, to be his wife.

For the next 40 years, this "prince" Moses helped take care of the flock of Jethro, his father-in-law, in the "back of the desert." Then as God heard the groanings of the Jewish slaves in Egypt, He sent an angel that appeared to Moses in a flame of fire from the midst of a bush (Ex. 3:2). From the burning bush, God called out, "Moses, Moses! ... Take your sandals off your feet, for the place where you stand *is* holy ground. ... Behold, the cry of the children of Israel has come to Me, and I have also seen the oppression with which the Egyptians oppress them. ... Come now, therefore, and I will send you to Pharaoh that you may bring My people, the children of Israel, out of Egypt" (Ex. 3:4,5,9,10).

Moses began to make excuses that he had a speaking

impediment, and finally God told him, He would also use his brother Aaron to help him. God gave to them supernatural signs, such as a rod that turned into a serpent, plagues of blood, frogs, lice, flies, diseased livestock, boils, hail, locusts, darkness, and death of the firstborn. After trying to evoke all sorts of compromises from Moses and Aaron without success, Pharaoh, following the death of the firstborn of every Egyptian family that did not have blood on their doorposts, allowed the Jewish slaves to leave.

But scarcely had they gone, than Pharaoh and his army relented, speeding after them. By now the Israelites were at the Red Sea. As they cried out to God, He drove back the waters so the Jews crossed on dry land. But when Pharaoh with his army followed them, the Red Sea swept over them, drowning all of them.

In the desert, God miraculously fed the nearly three million Jews and their cattle with manna from heaven, which appeared on the ground daily for six days each week. Yet the people complained again and again, even threatening to return to Egypt, and in another instance, to stone Moses and Aaron.

When the people cried for meat, God sent them quail in such abundance they stuffed themselves, and the Lord sent a great plague upon them (Num. 11:33). When they begged for water, the Lord told Moses, "Strike the rock, and water will come out of it, that the people may drink" (Ex. 17:6). God kept His promise. At yet another time, at Meribah, there was no water, and the people complained again. Then the Lord said to Moses, "Speak to the rock before their eyes, and it will yield its water" (Num. 20:8). But by this time, Moses was so aggravated over their continual threats against him and his brother, that in anger, he "struck the rock twice with his rod; and the water came out abundantly, and the congregation and their animals drank" (ver. 11).

Moses' fit of anger cost him dearly! The Lord said, "Because you did not believe Me, to hallow Me in the eyes of the children of Israel, therefore you shall not bring this assembly into the land which I have given them" (ver. 12). God always keeps His promises, and besides, He has a very good memory!

When Israel arrived at Mt. Sinai, God called Moses to come to the top of that mountain, leaving Aaron in charge of the people below. There God gave Moses the Ten Commandments which were to govern His people forever. When Aaron felt his brother was staying too long on the mountaintop, he told the people to break off their gold earrings and bring them to him so he could fashion a golden calf. The next day, the people offered burnt offerings to the calf, ate and drank and caroused. God told Moses:

> "Go, get down! For your people whom you brought out of the land of Egypt have corrupted *themselves*. ... Now therefore, let Me alone, that My wrath may burn hot against them and I may consume them. And I will make of you a great nation." Then Moses pleaded with the LORD ... "Turn from Your fierce wrath, and relent from this harm to Your people. Remember Abraham, Isaac and Israel." ... So the LORD relented (Ex. 32:7,10-14).

At one point, Moses even offered to lay down his own life

to spare Israel from extermination (Ex. 32:32). When Moses saw the golden calf, he broke in pieces the two tablets of the Ten Commandments. Later, Moses returned to Mt. Sinai where he spent 40 days and nights without food or water, and God renewed the covenant with him on the tablets. The Lord, in addition, gave instructions to build the tabernacle, a place of worship, and added other laws to make Israel holy by observing them.

When Moses and the people arrived at the Jordan River, Moses sent 12 spies to check out the Promised Land. When the spies returned, they reported that the land flowed with milk and honey, and brought back some of the fruit as proof. But 10 of the spies declared the giants in the land were ferocious, and "we were like grasshoppers in our own sight, and so we were in their sight" (Num. 13:33). They then persuaded the Israelites not to proceed into Canaan Land, against the advice of the two other spies, Caleb and Joshua, who urged to immediately proceed. So angry were the people that they wanted to stone the two with stones (Num. 14:10).

Then the Lord told Moses that because the congregation had rejected Him, all Israelites 20 years old and above, except for Joshua and Caleb, would die in the wilderness. But the little ones, "whom you said would be victims, I will bring in, and they shall know the land which you have despised" (ver. 31). They were the "generation following."

So it was, that for the next 40 years, the Israelites wandered in the wilderness, until the last member of that condemned generation had died. Yes, the generation following would inherit and settle in the Promised Land.

Moses used those years to train Joshua and Caleb, as well

as the elders, officials and the army, for the leadership needed when they crossed over the Jordan. God, as promised, did not allow Moses to cross over into the Promised Land, but He did allow him to stand on top of Mt. Nebo on a clear day and view for himself that land. Aaron by now had died.

One of the final directives God gave to Moses, before He took him up to the mountain at age 120 to bury him (no man knew where — Deut. 34:6), was to, "Encourage him (Joshua), for he shall cause Israel to inherit it (the Promised Land)" (Deut. 1:38). Every leader needs to be encouraged!

Of Moses, the Scripture says, "His eyes were not dim nor his natural vigor diminished" (Deut. 34:7). Not bad for 120 years! A great leader!

Chapter Eight

Double It!

G ordon used to say, "Some people wear out my office carpet, coming to show me a list of all the great things they're going to do. But when I meet them five or 10 years later, they haven't even started."

There were two great men of the Bible a generation apart — Elijah and Elisha. The younger said, "Double it!"

The name Elijah means "My God is God Himself." Elijah apparently believed that, for his exploits were phenomenal! Though a lonely figure, he was the grandest and most romantic character Israel ever produced — the greatest of prophets who came on the scene with suddenness.

By the power of the Holy Spirit, Elijah ended a three-year drought, was fed by ravens, multiplied meal and oil, raised a boy from the dead, called fire from heaven, slew 450 prophets of Baal and 400 prophets of Asherah, ran a 30-mile foot race and made many miraculous utterances that came to pass, including dividing the Jordan River — some 16 miracles in all.

When it came time to leave this world, Elijah did not go the usual way — through dying. He walked to Gilgal — which means "circle." A lot of people stay at Gilgal: All their lives they go in circles. He next traveled to Bethel — "the house of God." Then on to Jericho — "a fragrant place." But Elijah's destiny was beyond the Jordan River.

With him was young Elisha, his attendee, disciple and his successor — an unknown plowman. God often selects an individual who seems to have little qualification for the Herculean task He has planned for him. That way God can get more glory from that yielded life.

Elisha means "God is Savior." He was drawn to Elijah and followed him closely. Earlier, Elijah did have a young heir-apparent following him. But after Elijah killed the false prophets, in a moment of panic and fear, he and this young, unnamed servant ran for their lives — all the way from Mt. Carmel to Beersheba in the south. Here the servant left him and is never heard from again.

Not so Elisha. He clung to Elijah, as together they walked to the Jordan. To test his protégé, Elijah advised him several times — at Gilgal, Bethel, and Jericho — to stay with the other young sons of the prophets. But Elisha insisted on accompanying him (II Ki. 2:6). At the Jordan River, Elijah took off his mantle (coat), rolled it up, and struck the water, which divided so the two crossed on dry land.

Now Elijah, in his final goodbye to Elisha, said, "Ask! What may I do for you, before I am taken away from you?" (ver. 9). Elisha's answer came quickly, "Please let a double portion of your spirit be upon me" (ver. 9). Quite a request!

But one more test. Replied Elijah, "You have asked a hard thing. *Nevertheless*, if you see me *when I am* taken from you, it shall be so for you; but if not, it shall not be *so*" (ver. 10). No room for distractions!

No, Elijah did not die. "Suddenly a chariot of fire *appeared* with horses of fire, and separated the two of them; and Elijah went up by a whirlwind into heaven" (ver. 11).

Elijah had performed 16 recorded miracles in the Bible, but Elisha was asking for a "double portion." When would be a good time to begin? Immediately!

Elisha picked up the coat his mentor had left behind and smote the water of the Jordan, saying, "Where *is* the LORD God of Elijah?" (ver. 14). What happened? The waters parted and Elisha crossed over.

How about all the other Bible school students — the sons of the prophets? They bowed to the ground before Elisha as they acknowledged, "The Spirit of Elijah rests on Elisha" (ver. 15). Revealing their lack of faith, they urged Elisha to send a team of 50 men to look in the mountains for Elijah, fearing he had been dropped by God somewhere en route to heaven. But after searching three days, Elijah was nowhere to be found, and the sons of the prophets were never heard from again.

What about young Elisha? He held the office of prophet in Israel for 55 years, duplicating many of the miracles Elijah had performed, even to the capturing of the entire Syrian army by striking them with blindness. He led them to Samaria where the king of Israel asked Elisha if he should kill them. Elisha's gracious response was, "You shall not kill *them*. ... Set food and water before them, that they may eat and drink and go to their master" (II Ki. 6:22).

Did Elisha get his request for the "double portion"? Indeed he did! The Bible records that 32 miracles were done through his ministry.

In fact, God added even an extra one to his credit! When Elisha died, he was laid to rest in a cave. Later raiding bands from Moab invaded the land. One day as the Israelites were burying a man, they suddenly spied a band of these raiders, and hurriedly put the corpse into the tomb of Elisha. When the dead man touched the bones of Elisha, the corpse "revived and stood on his feet" (II Ki. 13:21). Elisha had more of the anointing power of God in his death than many have while they live! Thirty-two miracles plus one!

Chapter Nine

Doggedness Can Win!

Caleb, the dogged one — the bold, passionate, impetuous young man. Yes, Caleb (which means dogged), named after his father and grandfather, is one of my favorite characters in the Bible. He was chosen as one of the 12 spies Moses sent to search out the land of Canaan in preparation for the settling of the several million Jews that God delivered from Egypt. (Some 250 times God promised the Canaanite land to the Israelites.)

When the 12 spies returned from the journey, 10 gave a negative report: "A land that devours its inhabitants, and all the people whom we saw in it *are* men of *great* stature. There we saw the giants (the descendants of Anak came from giants); and we were *like* grasshoppers in our own sight, and so we were in their sight" (Num. 13:32,33).

The Bible says, "For as he thinks in his heart, so is he" (Prov. 23:7). So the 10 spies showed where their problem lay. The result? "All the congregation lifted up their voices and cried, and the people wept that night. ... 'If only we had died in the land of Egypt! Or if only we had died in this wilderness!'" (Num. 14:1,2).

But Caleb and Joshua had another recommendation. They

immediately said, "Let us go up at once and take possession, for we are well able to overcome it" (Num. 13:30). When the Israelites plotted among themselves about returning to Egypt because of the evil report they heard from the other 10 spies, Caleb and Joshua tore their clothes in anguish.

Eventually, the Israelites moved in to occupy the God-promised land. But that whole generation of complainers and doubters died in the wilderness as a judgment, without ever seeing Canaan, with the exception of the faith-filled Caleb and Joshua.

When Moses was ready to go to his eternal reward, whom did he choose as his successor? It was Joshua. How about Caleb? What was his reaction to Moses' choice? He accepted the leadership of his "buddy" Joshua and worked for many years alongside him, helping conquer the territories. These qualities of humility, submissiveness, loyalty and cooperation are sometimes rare in leaders today. But Caleb had the people of Israel at heart. So he humbled himself.

When Caleb was 85 years old, he approached his "boss," Joshua, and asked him a favor. No, he didn't request a retirement pension so he could sit in a rocking chair the rest of his life, whittling away with his pocketknife on a piece of hardwood from the trees of Lebanon, and spinning tales of the glorious miracles of yesteryear to the youngsters around him. No, he was just getting his "second wind" at 85! He still remembered the beautiful hill country where the giant descendants of Anak lived.

So what was Caleb's request? Forty-five years after he had brought back a "good report" from Canaan, and after several years of faithfully working with Joshua, he had this to say:

> "I am this day, eighty-five years old. As yet I *am as* strong this day as on the day that Moses sent me; just as my strength *was* then, so now *is* my strength for war, both for going out and for coming in. (He didn't plan to die on the battlefield!) Now therefore, give me this mountain of which the LORD spoke in that day; for you heard in that day how the Anakim *were* there, and *that* the cities *were* great *and* fortified. It may be that the LORD *will be* with me, and I shall be able to drive them out as the LORD said." And Joshua blessed him (Happy Birthday), and gave Hebron to Caleb ... as an inheritance (Josh. 14:10-13).

Caleb went to work and drove out the three sons of Anak (Josh, 15:14; Judg. 1:10); he conquered Hebron and some of the surrounding territory.

Why was Caleb so blessed and used of God? The Bible says five times that Caleb "wholly followed the LORD" (Josh. 14:9). He was not named dogged in vain. He was that!

With that kind of testimony, it is no wonder Caleb was able to get his "second wind" at age 85!

Chapter Ten

Time to Let Go!

What woman would want to be in Hannah's place? Her husband, Elkanah, told her he loved her dearly, but his other wife, Peninnah, provoked her endlessly. And they had to share the same house!

To make bad matters worse, Peninnah bore Elkanah both sons and daughters. And when it was time to sacrifice to the Lord, Elkanah gave Peninnah and her children a portion so they could offer sacrifices, too. While Hannah, who couldn't seem to get pregnant, stood by and watched, her heart grieved, even though Elkanah gave her a "special" portion.

It happened year after year! The whole family, including both wives and Peninnah's children, wended their way from the mountains of Ephraim to Shiloh to offer sacrifices at the tabernacle. Hannah, with a heavy heart, traipsed along with the frolicking children and their spiteful mother.

When they would reach the tabernacle, Hannah would not be able to hold back her grief any longer. She would refuse to eat. Her husband rebuked her, asking her if he wasn't better than 10 sons. What could she say?

One year, Hannah went to the tabernacle to pray about her desperate situation. But then came another rebuke! The priest in charge, Eli, watched her as she prayed and wept in anguish. He noticed Hannah's lips moving but she was making no sound, so he accused her of being drunk!

How did Hannah respond? Did she let anger overtake her for his lack of discernment? No. She called him "my lord" (sir). She explained that she had been praying in anguish out of her deep sadness. Amazingly, Eli responded right this time. He told Hannah, "Go in peace, and the God of Israel grant your petition which you have asked of Him" (I Sam. 1:17).

Early the next morning, the family returned home. "In the process of time ... Hannah conceived and bore a son, and called his name Samuel, *saying*, 'Because I have asked for him from the LORD'" (ver. 20).

Can you imagine the joy that filled Hannah's life, as she caressed her child of promise? No doubt she thought about her vow to God constantly as she watched Samuel grow. Fortunately, according to the custom of the Jews, a child was not weaned until the age of 4 or 5, so she had time to love and play with him, as she taught him the ways of the Lord.

All too soon the day arrived! This year, she accompanied the rest of Elkanah's family, as she took Samuel to Shiloh, there to leave him forever with God and Eli. When they arrived at Shiloh, she showed little Samuel around the tabernacle and worshiped God with him until time for their parting. As she held little Samuel in her arms, she likely told him, "You are now a BIG boy! No longer will you drink from Mommy's breast. You will eat like a big man. You will sleep in your own bed from now on, and Mommy won't be there to tuck you in. Eli will take care of you now, but Mommy will come to see you each year and bring you new clothes. Mommy loves you. Goodbye, my darling."

With her heart still aching as she turned to walk away from her son, instead of being overcome with grief, she began to worship the Lord.

"My heart rejoices in the LORD; my horn is exalted in the LORD. I smile at my enemies, because I rejoice in Your salvation. No one is holy like the LORD, for *there is* none besides You, nor *is there* any rock like our God. Talk no more so very proudly; let no arrogance come from your mouth, for the LORD *is* the God of knowledge; and by Him actions are weighed. The bows of the mighty men *are* broken, and those who stumbled are girded with strength. *Those who were* full have hired themselves out for bread, and the hungry have ceased *to hunger*. Even the barren has borne seven, and she who has many children has become feeble. The LORD kills and makes alive; He brings down to the grave and brings up. The LORD makes poor and makes rich; He brings low and lifts up. He raises the poor from the dust *and* lifts the beggar from the ash heap, to set *them* among princes and make them inherit the throne of glory. For the pillars of the earth *are* the LORD'S, and He has set the world upon them. He will guard the feet of His saints, but the wicked shall be silent in darkness. For by strength no man shall prevail. The adversaries of the LORD shall be broken in pieces; from heaven He will thunder against them. The LORD will judge the ends of the earth. He will give strength to His king, and exalt the horn of His anointed." Then Elkanah went to his house at Ramah. But the child minis- tered to the LORD before Eli the priest (I Sam. 2:1-11).

Yes, Hannah could have felt she had a right to renege on her covenant with God, for Eli had raised several ungodly sons. And what about Samuel — still so young to be away from his family? But Hannah's covenant was not with Eli; it was with God. Despite the special bond between this mother and her son, she kept her pledge. Knowing it was now needful, she released her son to God. The time to let go had arrived. And God used Samuel exceedingly in his lifetime.

In return for her gift of Samuel to Him, God honored Hannah, giving her three more sons and two daughters (ver. 21) — a bountiful harvest.

Chapter Eleven

A Loser Becomes a Winner

Saul was a brilliant, highly-educated Jew who studied under the famous Gamaliel, a Roman citizen, yet had great animosity against the believers in Jesus. He participated in their arrests and even in some being stoned to death.

But one day Saul, "still breathing threats and murder against the disciples of the Lord," was on his way to Damascus so that "if he found any who were of the Way, whether men or women, he might bring them bound to Jerusalem" (Acts 9:1,2).

While Saul was on this journey to Syria, God spoke to him: "Saul, Saul, why are you persecuting Me? ... I am Jesus, whom you are persecuting" (ver. 4,5). Saul fell to the ground; and being directed to the home of a believer (Ananias) in Damascus, he there accepted Jesus as His Messiah and was filled with the Holy Spirit. Jesus told Ananias that Paul was "a chosen vessel of Mine to bear My name before Gentiles, kings, and the children of Israel" (ver. 15).

After spending some years in the desert communicating with the Lord, Saul began his missionary journeys with measurable success. From this time on, he was referred to as "Paul." On his first journey, Paul was with the stalwart Barnabas and the young John Mark. As a young beginner, John Mark should have been thrilled to be selected to travel with the first missionaries, Paul and Barnabas.

But though God blessed the trio with marvelous miracles of salvation and healings, persecution and opposition met them in every city. Perhaps young John Mark didn't relish sleeping in unfamiliar places and eating "cold bread" when he could have enjoyed his mother's homecooking, slept in his own warm bed, and had clean clothes to wear. Whatever the reason, he opted to leave the party and go home — a deserter in Paul's eyes.

Later Paul asked Barnabas to go with him to see how the churches they had started were doing. Barnabas insisted on taking along his cousin (Col. 4:10), John Mark, who had deserted them on the last trip.

Paul was adamant. "No way!" The controversy became so strong that Paul and Barnabas parted company. Paul chose to take Silas, while Barnabas and his cousin sailed for Cyprus. (Sometimes in God's omniscient ways, multiplication can result by dividing, and increasing by decreasing.)

But what had happened to young John Mark earlier when he had left Paul and Barnabas? No doubt he headed straight for home — Jerusalem. What awaited him there?

Peter gives us a clue by where he immediately went after an angel helped him escape from prison: "the house of Mary, the mother of John whose surname was Mark, where many were gathered together praying" (Acts 12:12).

Yes, John Mark had a praying mother to greet him the day

he returned home as a defeated, depressed young evangelist — a failure. No doubt this mother clung to the words of Paul who preached, "Believe on the Lord Jesus Christ, and you will be saved, you and your household" (Acts 16:31).

So what happened to John Mark? We don't have all the details of his maturing in the Lord. However, we know it took place; later, when Paul was in prison in Rome, he wrote Timothy: "Get Mark and bring him with you, for he is useful to me for ministry" (II Tim. 4:11). When he wrote the Colossians, Paul sent greeting to "Mark, the cousin of Barnabas (about whom you received instructions: if he comes to you, welcome him)" (4:10). So Paul recommended Mark to the Colossian church.

John Mark's greatest achievement? He wrote the New Testament book of Mark that has blessed multiplied millions in the past two millenniums!! One can sense his impetuous nature in his writings as he constantly uses "immediately, at once, and again," etc.

Yes, John Mark, a failure, got his "second wind" and became a success!

Part III: Stories of Contemporary World Changers

Chapter Twelve

Little People
With a Big God!

To my late husband, Gordon, the Lord's command to "Go into all the world and preach the gospel to every creature" (Mk. 16:15), included the youth of the next generation. To train leaders to reach them meant schools — Bible schools. So his first such initiative was in Bangkok, Thailand from where he had met a Christian gentleman who begged for assistance to build a school.

Gordon helped raise funds to send his brother-in-law, Rev. Leon Hall, an Assembly of God pastor for many years, and Rev. Don Price, a fine musician and preacher, to Bangkok. For months they labored alongside the nationals to build a large school. It was completed in 1957. Years later, I was privileged to visit that school, where 1,000 students are being taught daily the truths of the Bible.

It was in 1970 that God laid it on Gordon's heart to take another step. He founded Christ For The Nations Institute in a former nightclub in Dallas, Texas. Fifty students enrolled. It was a difficult year. And when two leading teachers of only four resigned to start their own school in the city, taking some of our best students, suggestions were rampant to close our school. That summer, after fasting and praying, Gordon announced to me that CFNI would continue.

The following year, among the 125 students was a typical worldly young lady from New Jersey. Her name was Kay Humburg. When summer vacation came, she returned to the home of her parents, Bob and Emma Humburg. They saw such a change in Kay, they began to seek God for their own lives.

Bob, then father of three, had been an addictive gambler and an alcoholic. When he finally lost all control of his life, he deserted Emma and the children and hit the road to nowhere. One night at 3 a.m. in a dingy hotel room, holding a gun in his hand, he decided to "blow out my brains." Then, without knowing why, he reached over to turn on a radio. When he heard a preacher say, "Do you want to start a new life? Jesus can give you a new heart," Bob ripped open his old, dirty shirt and cried, "Yes, I want a new life," as he confessed his sin to God.

Bob headed for home. When he knocked at the door, Emma, who had become a Christian earlier, was reluctant even to let him in. He assured her he had found Jesus, but he had lied so often about so many things, could she believe him now? She did!

Bob became a new man, started attending church regularly with his family, and began paying his gambling debts and repaying employers from whom he had stolen. It took him eight years of steady employment to pay those debts.

Just about that time, Bob and Emma's oldest of four children, Kay, returned home from a year at Christ For The

Nations Institute. She was a changed young woman. As Bob and Emma began to seek God about their future, they felt impressed to "sell everything and attend CFNI with your entire family."

In August 1972, the Humburg family, now six in number, arrived on campus, and four of them — Bob, Emma, Kay and Lynn — enrolled in CFNI. The two younger ones attended later when they were old enough to qualify.

Soon Bob, showing signs of leadership, was elected president of his class. He and his family were in the Sunday afternoon service on April 1, 1973 when Gordon, while seated on the platform, suffered a heart attack and instantly went to be with the Lord.

The following year while working with the youth at CFNI, Bob, of German ancestry, Emma, and two of their daughters felt a call to Germany. That summer the whole family went to Germany, where Bob scoured that nation looking for a possible site for a Bible school. He and Emma returned to Dallas with several locations as possibilities, but as we studied them, we realized the costs were prohibitive.

"Stay here, Bob, and lead our student outreaches for another year, and let us be much in prayer during that time," I suggested. So Bob and Emma did just that, while Kay and Lynn, with another CFNI graduate named Lynn, stayed in Germany. There they rented a room in a private home, where without heat and with very little money, they fasted and prayed for one year. Much prayer that year ascended to God, from Dallas as well.

It was now the summer of 1974. Bob and Emma left a second time for Germany to look for a building site. Drawn to the Wolfenbüttel area near Braunschweig, a city of 250,000, Bob contacted a real estate agent. The very first building the agent showed him was a large former soap factory built in 1902. Later Hitler had appropriated it to train his SS leaders; a permanent swastika was engraved over the door. Then it was purchased by a chemical manufacturer; but after this company merged with another in Switzerland, the building was left vacant for three years. When Bob first saw it, he thought it was too big.

We flew our Dallas business administrator, Norman Young, to negotiate the price: To replace it would cost $2 million; but the Lord was with us. We bought the factory for $152,000, interest free, with only $2,000 down! It was a two-story building with 45,000 square feet of floor space.

Renovation began immediately with a dozen or so CFNI graduates assisting to construct a 350-seat auditorium. We gave them free room and board for their work.

In 1976, during April, May and June, a mini, three-month Bible school was launched with 18 students, who were, as Bob called them, "broken down young people." That fall, September 1976, the first one-year Bible school was opened with 30 students. Students and staff all lived and worked in this building appropriately named Glaubenszentrum — Faith Center. Food and housing was promised and provided for everyone.

The next 12 years were a time of growth and testing and laying a firm Christ-honoring foundation. About 90 students enrolled for the second year. As the attendance grew, a large 80-room apartment complex was purchased for a dormitory and staff housing. But when month-end conferences began to be held, the 350-seat auditorium was no longer large enough to hold the crowds. A roomier facility was needed. But where?

Again Bob approached the real estate agent, by now his good friend. Just 45 miles from their location in Wolfenbüttel and also from the large city of Hanover, a huge school (that Hitler had earlier built and personally dedicated to train his elite drivers and officers) was up for sale. After Hitler's decease, the German government had been using it to train West German border guards, but decided to merge them with trainees in another part of Germany. Now these fabulous, expansive buildings in Bad Gandersheim were for sale! We learned the replacement cost was about $5 million (U.S.). Then word came to us the government would sell them to us for about $1.3 million.

So we had to sell our two other buildings for cash. God worked another miracle. The city of Wolfenbüttel bought the original school from us and paid cash; the apartment building was also sold for cash. So we were home free!

Then to our great surprise, when the city of Wolfenbüttel began to dig to lay a foundation for their Community Youth Center on the location where our former Bible school stood, they had to remove a depth of 20 feet of soil from the entire area! They learned the ground had been contaminated, no doubt, by the chemical company that had owned and operated there before we bought it.

Thus in May 1987, we purchased this mammoth, colossal, beautiful property, perched on top of a high hill overlooking the resort town of Bad Gandersheim. When Bob first saw it he knew it was too big. "Not so," God told him.

Excitement knew no bounds, both in Germany with the

staff and students, as well as on our Dallas campus, as we earnestly sought God's guidance. The move was major, and we realized the additional cost would require more miracles. Again God answered our joint prayers.

Bob and Emma were approaching retirement age. Who could oversee the ministry of this now far-reaching Bible school?

While attending Christ For The Nations Institute in Dallas, Kay had met another student, Mike Chance. Who was Mike? His father had deserted the family when Mike was two, and had later died. Mike had run away from home in California at age 14. His mother and grandmother tried to raise him but he fell in with the hippie culture which led him into drugs. Later he joined the U.S. Marines.

In the providence of God, Mike started attending Chuck Smith's church in Costa Mesa, and there he accepted Jesus as Lord and Savior. His next move was to enroll at CFNI in Dallas and get soundly rooted and grounded in the Lord during the next two years.

After graduation, Mike went to Germany as one of the volunteers who worked to help renovate our new Bible school in Wolfenbüttel. There Kay and Mike renewed their friendship, courted for a time, and were eventually married. They have been a guiding, stable light from the inception of the German Bible school — anointed, chosen leaders.

Mike is a powerful preacher, teacher (speaking in German as well as English), and worship leader. He has led the Christians in the annual *Germany for Jesus* parade. He and Kay have three children — two lovely daughters and a young son. His eldest daughter, Catherine, is now on staff assisting in the work of the German Bible school, while Joy is presently attending CFNI in Dallas.

Today the German school, like our Dallas institute, offers a two-year as well as a three-year program; nearly 200 German-speaking students come from all over Europe. At the month-end conferences, a popular addition, all facilities are packed out. This necessitated additional housing. Thus, a scenic hotel five minutes away was purchased and is already paid for.

This past year, a state-of-the-art 1,200-seat auditorium was built on the campus. It was the privilege of our Dallas tour group to be present at the very first service held in that auditorium in May 1998, during which I was honored to bring the commencement address.

In the past few weeks, 629 men met in that auditorium for the first men's conference led by Mike Chance. On an earlier weekend, 1,000 ladies held their women's conference led by Kay Chance.

Kay is also a songwriter, having composed many beautiful songs and choruses, including *Ah, Lord God*, which is being sung around the world to God's glory.

In 1998, Mike was appointed executive director of Europe for Christ For The Nations' Associated Bible schools. He will serve as a regional overseer of our associate schools in Belarussia, Bulgaria, England, Germany, Moldova, Romania and the Ukraine.

The end is not yet in sight. As Bob Humburg, the founder, told me recently, this work is the result of "little people with a great big God." The next generation is carrying on!

Chapter Thirteen

Taking Ground From Satan

G ordon used to say, "Every day, I drive the devil back a little further."

A letter from Ezekiel and Eunor Guti:

"Forward in Faith Ministries began on May 12, 1960 under a gum tree in Zimbabwe; many miracles of healing took place. In 1971 when the church grew to 80, the Lord sent me to Christ For The Nations Institute in Dallas for more Bible training. Gordon Lindsay was my teacher, and in him, I saw the character of Jesus. He taught in a very simple way that made it easy to understand and to impart to others. Even today, I still remember what he taught me.

"After graduation in May 1972, I expected to get funds in America to support my Forward in Faith pastors in Zimbabwe, but that did not work out. Instead I got a firm foundation and the knowledge of the Word. Then the Lord told me to go back and faithfully teach His Word to His people in Africa. I began to share with others all I had learned, including the teaching on giving. My people started to give.

"I saw poor folk who had nothing, who used empty tins of cooking oil for chairs, who slept on the floor, and some who didn't even have shoes, begin to prosper. Women who used to sit around doing nothing except gossip and beg for money, began through self-help projects to work with their hands and support the ministry. The Lord continued to bless them and raise them up. Even until today, there are no more lazy women, and the Lord is blessing them as they help the ministry. They are now the backbone of the church, financially.

"Outstanding miracles continue to happen wherever I preach. Many blind receive sight, many crippled are healed, hundreds have been delivered from evil spirits, and childless women have borne children. Through these miracles, the church has grown fast and has become one of the largest in the country. We have Bible schools all over the land — three day schools and 50 evening ones — plus a correspondence school.

"Within our work there is a diversity of ministries in an effort to reach all people with the Word of God so they may be saved:

An orphanage center.

A child evangelism ministry, which is very large.

A university campus students' ministry.

"We go into all schools and colleges preaching Jesus to the youth and children. In our ministry to the blind, we train some of them to be pastors among the blind; likewise, we train the handicapped to be pastors among the handicapped. In a ministry to the executives — men and women — we focus on marriage. In hundreds of dressmaking schools, we train women to operate their own businesses; the business people, we train how to run businesses. God is blessing, and some have become Christians. Several of our pastors are chaplains in the army and some in the police force. In addition, our adult literacy and nursery school programs reach people of all walks of life.

"Our ministry has spread and we have churches in Mozambique, Botswana, Zambia, South Africa, Lesotho, Tanzania, Namibia, Angola, Kenya, Democratic Republic of Congo, Ghana, Swaziland, Ethiopia, Malawi, Rwanda, Australia, England, Scotland and Germany. In these nations, altogether, we have 4,000 churches and over 3,000 pastors. By the grace of God, we have managed to build more church buildings than any national organization. Our God is a very good God.

"I thank the Lord for the teachings of Christ For The Nations Institute, for the late Gordon Lindsay, and for Freda Lindsay, who took up the mantle and became a model to leaders young and old. My wife, Eunor, and I admire the life and determination in her. Eunor admires the faith Freda has needed to raise funds for that ministry. We praise God as we see Dennis catching the mantle from his father and mother."

(Eunor remained in Zimbabwe to watch over the ministry while Ezekiel attended CFNI. Upon his return home, however, he took a cassette to her of my teaching on how to minister the baptism in the Holy Spirit [see Chapter 27]. After playing it several times, she told Ezekiel, "I can do that!" He replied, "Then do it!" She did. By holding women's meetings not only in Zimbabwe but also in the neighboring countries, many thousands have been filled with the Holy Spirit under her teaching, for which we praise God!)

Chapter Fourteen

A Lawyer? President? Rabbi? "Lord, What?"

W ith a smile on his face, Gordon used to say, "Up to now it's worked!" when an individual asked him to explain some of the seemingly outlandish promises Jesus gave to believers.

Scott Hinkle — born to a Jewish couple on St. Patrick's day, 1951 in Neptune, New Jersey — can say the same.

With his maternal grandparents in show business in the early 20th century, it was natural for Scott to have a great interest in music. He studied the trumpet and played drums. At age 13, Scott had his bar mitzvah, after completing the required special training in Hebrew and Judaism. It was Scott's feeling that his family attended the reform synagogue only to train up their children in that faith.

With Abraham Lincoln as his boyhood idol, Scott dreamed of going to Princeton University, becoming a lawyer, and eventually being the first Jewish president of the United States. Or maybe a rabbi. All of his dreams of greatness were supported by his parents and grandmother.

In the good-sized Jewish community in which Scott grew

up, there was also a sizeable Italian population. During his teen years, some of Scott's friends began to dress and act like gangsters so they would "look cool." Alcohol and drugs flowed freely in this circle, and soon Scott became addicted to heroin, shattering his big dreams.

After being arrested by police on heroin charges, Scott was admitted to a psychiatric ward. His lawyer entered a plea bargain: Scott would receive probation if, in addition to continuing psychiatric care and returning to school, he would leave the state of New Jersey. He agreed and went to live with relatives in Kansas.

One week after Scott's 19th birthday, he attended an early morning mandatory high school assembly in Great Bend, Kansas. This assembly featured an "anti-drug lecture, given by a former drug user and Hollywood rock musician, Charles McPheeters. This Charles told his life story, and at the very end mentioned it was Jesus Christ Who had delivered him from drugs."

Scott was sitting in the balcony with a distant cousin who also used drugs. Scott was not interested, and while Charles spoke, he was making fun of him. "All of a sudden," says Scott, "something brushed across my face and a voice (like a quiet but firm thought in one's mind) spoke to me saying, 'Listen to him. This guy has something to say. You don't know everything.'" While Scott's mind quickly began manufacturing excuses why not to listen to McPheeters, his heart kept telling him what he was hearing was the truth.

Like a magnet, Scott felt drawn to this man. But McPheeters left quickly after that session as he had two more assemblies in other cities in which to speak that day. Scott quickly borrowed a car and caught up with Charles in a community 20 miles away. Together they went to a root-beer stand. It was then that Scott, who said he didn't know how to pray, made the "big decision."

Simply bowing his head in the front seat of a 1969 red and white Malibu Chevy, Scott silently called out to God, praying, "Lord, if You can do all that this guy is talking about, then go on ahead and do it, because it is either You or the gutter, and I have been in the gutter!"

Immediately, he felt as if Someone had come into him with a scrub brush and a hose and was cleaning him up from the inside. It felt like all the garbage and crud drained out of his life. A few months later, Scott received the infilling of the Holy Spirit and was healed of his physical infirmities.

Within hours, Scott began telling his friends what had happened to him, testifying, "Jesus loves you; He changed my life, and I don't do drugs anymore. Don't knock Him until you try Him."

His conversion was so dramatic that an article was written in a high school newspaper documenting the change in his life. Doors began to open for Scott to speak in churches, youth groups, Full Gospel Businessmen's meetings, etc. This was during the peak of the Jesus Movement, and Scott found himself entering right into ministry.

It was in 1971 that McPheeters urged Scott to attend a new Bible school in Dallas called Christ For The Nations Institute. Scott says of the two years he attended, "The Word of God and the ministry of the Holy Spirit had a drastic affect on both my personal life and ministry as well. That December, while praying about my future and ministry, I sensed the

Holy Spirit impressing Matthew 4:23 on my heart: 'And Jesus went about all Galilee, teaching in their synagogues, preaching the gospel of the kingdom, and healing all kinds of sickness and all kinds of disease among the people.' This became a cornerstone passage of the Bible, identifying God's call to itinerant evangelism. The time at this Bible school laid a good foundation in both ministry and my life with the building blocks of prayer, faith, integrity, God's Word and soulwinning."

After Scott graduated from CFNI, he later told me, "Mom Lindsay, in the very first service in which I spoke to a group of young people, I used your 'recipe' on how to minister the baptism in the Holy Spirit. A dozen of them were filled that night!"

Scott, as an associate director, helped Charles and Judy McPheeters establish a multifaceted street ministry in Hollywood called the Holy Ghost Repair Service.

In the meantime, Scott prayerfully selected as his wife, Nancy, a CFNI alumna, who has been a tremendous blessing and strength in their joint ministry. Their two children, Donovan and Stephanie, are an added gift from the Lord to reach the youth.

In 1981, the Hinkles launched their own association as a vehicle to facilitate evangelistic crusades and outreaches across the U.S., calling it Scott Hinkle Outreach Ministries (SHOM). Every year since, SHOM has spearheaded an outreach to the Mardi Gras in New Orleans. This team averages 100 plus workers each year and is made up of men and women from across America.

In Scott's National Street Ministries Conferences,

founded in 1984, thousands of men and women have been trained for frontline evangelism throughout America and even overseas.

Nancy co-leads a monthly women's discipleship mini-seminar in the inner city at Los Angeles' International Church/Dream Center. She also travels, ministering in retreats, conferences and churches, plus overseeing the offices of SHOM.

Currently, the Hinkles' ministry is based in Phoenix, Arizona, where they are members of Tommy Barnett's First Assembly of God.

In 1986, Nancy was diagnosed with cancer. Scott reports, "In between two surgical operations the cancer disappeared. The doctors could not find the cancer they had discovered earlier. The Great Physician, Jesus Christ, had performed a miracle. To this day no trace of cancer has ever been found in her body! Nancy and my own ministry moved up to a new level of usefulness as a result. To God be all the glory!"

"Yes, Lord, Your call was and is best for our lives," say Scott and Nancy Hinkle.

"Up to now, it's worked!"

Chapter Fifteen

"Benson, You're on Your Own!"

Benson! How would someone with his background, determination and purpose turn out? I was moved with pity and compassion when I learned the facts.

Born of John and senior wife, Sarah Idahosa, who were heavy into juju worship, sacrificing to idols, reincarnation, and witchcraft, it seemed that Benson, a sickly child, had little chance of being used by God.

Besides that, John hated Benson and considered him a curse because of his fragility and his inexplicable fainting spells. So he ordered Sarah to get rid of this 18-month old son at once by disposing of him on the garbage dump about 100 yards away. Sarah seemed to have no choice: obey her husband's command or leave.

On this particular night, Benson had another fainting spell; so sorrowfully, Sarah wrapped her child in her arms and headed for the pile of refuse, knelt beside it, and weeping softly, laid the motionless bundle on the pile of rubbish. Slowly, she returned to her house.

Several hours passed, when suddenly flashes of lightning

streaked across the sky and the rain poured noisily on the corrugated tin roof. But above the turmoil, Sarah heard the wail of a baby! Could it be that Benson had revived? She must find out. So through the dark, stormy night she headed for the dump as the cries of her child grew louder. Picking him up, she held the soaked child to her breast and carried him to their house.

When John realized what his wife had done, his rage knew no end. Sarah decided to pack up a few things and together, she and Benson would go to live with her parents. There Sarah worked in the yam harvest to help support the two. As time went on, she noticed that Benson's fainting spells had diminished and that he was growing — even a little taller than other children his age. John came on several occasions to visit them, and she was proud to show off Benson to him. When Benson was four, Sarah and he moved back with John, who by then was a timber contractor and the high priest of the juju for the Idahosa family.

When Benson was 8 years old, his mother enrolled him in an Anglican missions school and convinced John to pay the 15-cents-a-month fee. But after only one year, John moved his family again — this time to a place where there was no school at all. Later, when another move was made, Benson did get a second year of school.

At age 11, his father introduced him to two men who took Benson to his uncle Joseph's farm to work. His job was to help sow and harvest groundnuts, yams, cassava, okra and other crops. So while Joseph's children went to school, Benson worked long hours in the fields. The one bright spot in his life was that he was able to look on as his cousins did their homework and learn to read from their schoolbooks.

Soon it was Christmas time. Joseph had bought all of his children clothes, shoes, etc.; he had even bought a shirt for Benson. But when the gifts were passed around, Benson did not get the shirt — which would have been his very first Christmas gift. Uncle Joseph told him he was withholding the gift, for he had found some weeds Benson should have pulled in one of the crops. A couple of years went by, but each Christmas, Benson was deprived of his gift for some minor infraction.

When Benson was 16 years old, his paternal grandmother in Benin City invited him to live with her. She agreed to pay Benson's fees at the Methodist boarding school. Each day when classes were over, Benson worked in the hot, crowded kitchen of a little hotel his grandparents owned. But his great love was school and the books he consumed.

At age 18, Benson had saved enough to buy his first pair of shoes, and here came Benson's first exposure to the true Gospel. The local pastor befriended him and led him to Jesus, Who became his Lord and Savior.

Shortly, his grandfather introduced Benson to the manager of the Bata Shoe Company, who hired him to work in the stock room. Benson applied himself and received promotion after promotion.

One day Benson received a phone call from his mentor, British missionary Elton, who said that Gordon Lindsay was coming to Benin City. Earlier Benson had received a copy of *Christ For The Nations* magazine, in which a correspondence course was mentioned. He wrote to Gordon and received a packet of books and study materials.

When Gordon met Benson in Benin City, he invited him to attend his new school called Christ For the Nations Institute in Dallas and offered him a work scholarship.

By now, Benson had married Margaret, a bright, charming young woman whom he had led to the Lord. He had also won several of his family members and was actually pastoring a church. He was able to take a leave of absence from Bata Shoe Company with full pay in order to support Margaret while he was studying in Dallas.

That was 1971. I wrote at the time: "I first saw him when he walked one day into the classroom of 125 students at Christ For The Nations Institute." (The school was only in its second year, and classes were held in a former nightclub.) Someone said to me, "He's Benson Idahosa, our first student from Nigeria."

There he stood, a young black man, 30 years of age — tall, thin, meticulously dressed. I watched as he spoke to his classmates. That he was a very intense person was immediately apparent. He dominated the conversation. "A natural-born leader," I thought. I did not know he had once been a sickly infant, left on a rubbish heap to die.

At CFNI he was a bundle of activity. His natural charisma opened weekend speaking opportunities to him that would never have come to the average student. But Benson was not average in any sense of the word. Yet he seemed to carry a tremendous weight of some kind. At times he would weep out loud while a teacher was speaking. What was wrong? Or right? It turned out he was weeping for the souls of lost and dying mankind.

One day, Gordon asked me, "Have you noticed how

Benson prays?" I had indeed. "When he returns to his own land, he'll be heard from," Gordon added. Benson felt he just could not take out two years from his African responsibilities to complete the course at CFNI, so he left early. Later on, the institute conferred upon him its associate of practical theology degree in recognition of his outstanding and far-reaching work for the Lord.

Before leaving CFNI, Benson shared his vision with Gordon and me: to build a large center and school "like CFNI." (He hadn't told us he had already measured the CFN headquarters building and found it to be 200 feet long.) "We'll help you put on the roof," we promised him.

Not long after my husband's homegoing I received pictures from Benson of a huge foundation with walls just started. "What does Benson think he's doing?" I exclaimed. "You don't start that big. I'll write and tell him to cool it."

But the Holy Spirit whispered, *"Leave him to me. Write and encourage him and renew your commitment to him."* So I did, thinking it would be a long time — at least several years — before he would be ready for that roof.

But to my surprise, before the year was out, Benson wrote, "Dear Mom, we're ready for the roof. Come and see!" So on a missions trip to Africa, I visited Benin City. What a sight! I spoke at the dedication service. That Sunday, there were about 6,000 people present. We worshiped in a building that had only huge palm branches for a roof to shade us from the scorching sun. Yes, Benson was ready for the roof. We kept our commitment and sent him $46,000. The church was 201 feet long. Benson beat us by one foot.

That was just the beginning! His work began to expand.

Not long after, Benson wrote me that he was building a new Miracle Center seating 10,000. He wanted a commitment that we would again help him financially.

This time I wrote him, "Benson, you are on your own!" To continue to underwrite this and other of his projects, I felt would stymie the faith he needed to develop in order to be used in God's full plan for him.

Benson, on his own, did build that 10,000 seat Miracle Center, as well as a huge international headquarters for the All Nations For Christ Bible School; a Word of Faith group of schools; a nursery and primary school; a Word of Faith college; a Dental Faith mediplex and male and female dorms for it; lecture halls for his Christian Faith University; a multipurpose auditorium; and hundreds of churches all over Nigeria. How important it was to help him step into the deep!

Benson's television program reached millions, both in Africa and in the United States. As he became internationally known, he was sought out as a speaker in conferences in many nations.

God called him home on Sunday, April 5, 1998, at age 60. His work goes on under the leadership of Margaret, his wife and successor, and his family — the next generation following!

Chapter Sixteen

Adventure of a Lifetime

... In the Heart of the Former U.S.S.R.!
A letter from David Brunk:

Outside, it was freezing. Biting winds, too. We were in the heart of the former Soviet Union — Minsk, Belarus. And inside the cramped apartment that doubled as our office, it wasn't much better. The temperature was slightly warmer, but a different kind of cold gripped everyone gathered around our small broken table. As we reviewed our situation, we counted 10 things — 10 "processes," happening all at once — each of which had the power to close our doors, within the next 24 hours. No exaggeration. Each, in fact, could have/should have closed down what had taken years to build. Christ For The Nations-Belarus had quickly become the largest Bible institute in the nation; and that made us a target.

The night before, the KGB had been to the building where we held our classes and they wanted answers. Who were we? What were we doing? Soon afterwards, remote cameras mysteriously appeared, facing our doors. One of our greatest friends, a scientist who allowed us to use his empty classrooms each evening, directed us to the hallway where we could "safely talk." He feared there were listening devices in his office. In a whisper, he warned us that our situation was "bad." But he stayed with us — at great personal risk — till his death several years later.

Technically, we were legal. We had submitted all the proper documents. We had even openly stated our "religious nature." But in Belarus, the state of being legal depends more on relationships and favor than it does on documents. The larger we grew, the more difficult this became.

We ultimately came to an important understanding: To survive, we would not be able to stay hidden. We needed to become real servants if we were to find real, lasting favor. Tremendous needs confronted us daily in this country that was dealing with 70 percent of the nuclear fallout from Chernobyl. But thanks to special friends like those of Global Assistance, the Belarussian Children's Fund, Josh McDowell Ministries, From the Heart, the CIS Foundation, even the U.S. Embassy, the doors have remained open. We still retain a good relationship — with neighbors and government.

Back to that day around the table. Little did we know how radical we seemed — especially within the church community. Everything we did was different — the students we accepted, our curriculum, the way we taught, the level of spiritual emphasis — and controversial. And none more than our worship. The contemporary move of praise and worship was just coming to the CIS, and in our first class of 40 students, there was a pianist and a singer with the Philharmonic, and several music teachers. What happened when these terrific talents met the Spirit of God was simply ordained of the Lord. These highly trained musicians loved spontaneous, free worship. The presence of Jesus was so strong — night after night after night!

But it was all so new in those early days. The now deceased Bishop Marchuck, truly a great man of God, first brought us under his protection. Soon he began to receive tremendous criticism and pressure to remove us. We learned we might be asked to leave his spiritual and legal covering, and without it, we would be forced to leave the country.

And then there was the minister of religion. I had been to his office a week earlier to report our activities and try to build a relationship. But he was not impressed. We were a foreign organization, and he felt we should leave the country. Rather than have him just show up sometime, we invited him to be our guest lecturer for an evening on the current religious laws of Belarus. We first introduced him to our office staff. He questioned only two people — both Belarussian musicians on our worship team, and he was impressed at their level of education. This would soon be important.

That night, he witnessed a special worship encounter with Jesus, and was so touched, that when he stood to lecture, all of his distance and suspicion were gone. Instead he began to share openly from his heart about his love for his country and his deep concern at how unprepared his nation was for the onslaught of unknown religions that were invading (and they were). He shared about the activities of a number of dangerous new religious groups that were at work in Belarus. He was not the only one who was changed that night. So were we.

We did not meet the enemy we had expected. After speaking for nearly an hour, the students spontaneously rose and gave him a standing ovation. As he left our auditorium, he entered the hallways of the building where we shared facilities with a scientific institute, and it turned out they were having a "disco" — drunkenness and screaming rock and roll — some of what troubled him in the nation he loved. He became another important friend in the days to come.

And then there was the ministry of education. They too were soon to reject our status as an official "institute." The issues were many and serious. A mountain of rules and regulations. The incompatibility of religion and education, as they saw it.

And then there were the local police; and problems with our office. A panel of Belarussian lawyers counseled foreign businessmen: "In the end the law (or lack of) may not be the most important issue. Laws are open to interpretation by each local police station. Better to make a friend." God gave us favor. And more miracles. And more friends.

Back around the broken table on that cold gloomy day, we did our best to encourage each other. This work was not ours. It was His, and nothing short of Jesus could keep it alive. We could only keep following Him. When we prayed one more time and left the room that difficult day, none of us could have imagined what God was about to accomplish.

After five intense years had settled, Christ For The Nations–Belarus had become:

- Among the largest Bible institutes in the nation;
- Among the largest humanitarian organizations in the nation;
- Among the largest producers and distributors of Christian music in the entire CIS;

- Host of a yearly worship symposium that gathers worship leaders from all the 11 time zones of the CIS;

- Owners of a building in the capital city of Minsk, and witnesses of the countless miracles it represents on both sides of the Atlantic. (Christ For The Nations-Belarus was the first foreign organization ever allowed to compete in an auction in Minsk — and against all odds and far richer organizations that wanted the property, we won.);

- Assisters of nearly 30 churches to receive funding through CFN's Native Church program;

- Disciplers of wonderful students who now shake their nation with the One who shook them in those wonderful evenings in His presence;

- Home of a wonderful family of committed brothers and sisters, now known as Christ For The Nations-Belarus!

The most wonderful blessing of all is the people that the Lord assembles together to become His body — a family!!!

A special note of appreciation to the very special friends who shouldered unique weights and helped establish who we are, and to all those who came and saw and gave and went home to silently support us. And to all those that have not seen, and yet believed and faithfully supported us for all these years.

Jesus said, "Behold, I am coming quickly, and My reward *is* with Me" (Rev. 22:12). Lord, You are our reward. With all our hearts we say, THANKS, LORD, IT'S BEEN GREAT ... BECAUSE YOU ARE GREAT!!!

Chapter Seventeen

Many Are Called — Some Are Chosen

Christ For The Nations Institute of Dallas is 29 years old. It was founded by my husband, Gordon Lindsay, in 1970. Some 26,000 of all ages have attended.

What are the backgrounds of these students? Some are businessmen or women, teachers, ministers, missionaries, youth or children's workers, housewives, laborers of every variety, doctors, dentists and lawyers.

Forrest Hood (Fob) James III had earned a bachelor of arts at the University of Virginia in 1979 and a law degree from Duke University in 1982.

But Fob, a born-again Christian, desired a knowledge of the Bible, God's Word, to give himself a strong foundation on which to build and pattern his life. He decided to move his wife and two children to Dallas to attend Christ For The Nations Institute for one semester.

At the close of that first semester, Fob felt he had just scratched the surface of the Bible, so he'd stay a second term. That time flew and he asked himself, "Why not a third?" He and his wife completed the third and continued through the fourth, finishing the two-year course.

Back to their home in Alabama they went. Fob's father would later run and win his second term as governor of that state.

On March 1, 1998 the *Birmingham News* wrote concerning young Fob: "During both of his father's gubernatorial terms, Forrest Hood James III has helped to shape the governor's message on what both view as the unwarranted, unconstitutional intrusions of federal courts into prayer and other matters that they say the states should regulate."

"Prayer is rendered to God, not to men. The Supreme Court, a mere human court, has no jurisdiction over us or authority to forbid it." These words were part of a 34-page letter to U.S. District Judge Ira Dement, who presided over a case involving school-sponsored religious activities in DeKalb County schools. The letter was signed by Governor Fob James, who wholeheartedly endorses the view that federal judges have no authority to rule on such matters as prayer in public schools, partial birth abortion or on an Etowah County judge's posting of the Ten Commandments in his courtroom.

But the words were penned by a Birmingham lawyer, Fob James III, and he believes them with a passion that rivals his father's. "He certainly has been the principal architect for our position on these issues," the former governor said recently.

"His interest in matters spiritual has been of long standing. And that interest has steered some of his career moves such as his attendance at Bible school at the Dallas-based Christ For The Nations."

"'He knows the Bible better than anybody that I know, and that includes some preachers,' said his cousin, Braxton Counts."

Birmingham News goes on to say: "If the younger James were willing to publicly discuss his unpaid legal work for his father and the principle at stake, he would put it like this: 'Nobody has ever taken this proclamation of superior wisdom on the part of the legal profession and communicated it to the masses and it's about 100 years overdue.'"

During the two years Fob lived on our campus, his mother, Bobbie James, came at times to visit him and his family. It was then we met and became personal friends. She would call me on occasion to pray over a need in her husband's political career, asking also at times for our students to join in prayer with them.

When Fob's dad was elected the Alabama governor for a second term, my son Dennis' wife, Ginger, and I flew to Montgomery for the inauguration. The Montgomery Symphony Orchestra played "Stand Up, Stand Up for Jesus," "Standing on the Promises," and "Onward Christian Soldiers." After the governor's acceptance speech, in which he so boldly upheld godliness and righteousness, I told Ginger that I felt as though we had just come from a revival meeting!

The following morning, Ginger and I were among a selected group of believers invited to the Governor's Mansion, where we sang together and dedicated the manse to the Lord.

Last year on the occasion of CFN's 50th Anniversary Conference, Governor Fob James Jr. of Alabama was one of our keynote speakers.

Would to God all 50 of our United States' governors honored the Lord as does Fob James Jr. of Alabama.

Chapter Eighteen

Two of the New Breed

Bonnie never wanted to be a missionary. Her roommates at Christ For The Nations Institute fasted and prayed over foreign countries and the call to go to the mission field, while Bonnie poured her life into music and the ministry of praise and worship. Then she met Tom.

Tom Deuschle was born in Denver, Colorado, in 1954, the eldest of eight children. His family was Catholic, and Tom was expected to become a Jesuit priest. The family was born again when Tom was in his late teens and in 1972, he, too, gave his life to the Lord. The first year, Tom began leading a youth group of over 200 teenagers. From this group, many came to CFNI, and more than 30 young people entered full-time ministry. After three years at a university, God directed Tom to attend CFNI in Dallas.

After graduating, Tom felt he had a clear call to Zimbabwe, Africa (Rhodesia at that time), which was in the midst of a bitter civil war. He survived on $100 per month support, while visiting many farming areas and experiencing first-hand God's protecting power.

After Zimbabwe's independence, Tom returned to CFN where he met his wife, Bonnie Laughlin, who was born in

Pennsylvania, the eldest of two daughters. She won several state awards for her singing; she played piano, French horn and trumpet, writing songs at age 12. After high school, Bonnie became a member of Fred Waring's "Blenders." After hearing the testimony of Miss America 1967, Bonnie gave her life to Jesus and devoted her music career to Him.

Bonnie later attended Oral Roberts University and was one of the World Action Singers, touring the U.S. with them and Richard Roberts and appearing weekly on television. After graduation and obtaining a degree in music education, Bonnie attended CFNI for further Bible training and study in praise and worship. Here she met and married Tom in 1980. Tom returned to Zimbabwe with his new bride.

Their first year was a time of great adjustments, especially for Bonnie, who dealt with culture shock, and married to someone almost a stranger and in a strange country! Almost immediately, God spoke to them to start a church; they held their first service in their home with six people. As the church grew, they rented an auditorium in 1982, and held their first service as Rhema Bible Church with 52 people. As they plunged into pastoring, teaching, counseling and administration, Tom's vision was to build a strong Word-based church in Harare, to meet the needs of people — spirit, soul and body — plus provide a base to reach Zimbabwe and the five surrounding nations of Central Africa.

That same year, with a congregation only 16 weeks old, the church purchased an old hotel, which became the "nerve center" — housing offices, counseling rooms, bookstore, tape library, youth ministry office and children's church. The congregation helped to renovate the building and gathered there for Bible studies and prayer meetings — even without chairs. But God was there!

Twelve hundred people attended their first faith seminar. Many found Jesus and many more were miraculously healed. At their first Covenant Women's Tea, over 100 ladies attended, including the Honorable Mrs. Canaan Banana, the wife of Zimbabwe's president. Today these teas, held three or four times yearly, are a highlight of their conferences, attracting thousands of women from all walks of life, who never attend church.

By 1984, the congregation of 500 opened their two-year Bible school. Today it is fully accredited and offers students a four-year bachelor of arts degree in theology and biblical studies, as well as supervised postgraduate studies for master's and doctoral programs.

The next year, Bonnie produced her first worship album, "You Mean Everything to Me." A year later, Tom and Bonnie became parents; they now have four sons and a daughter. In 1987, Bonnie held a national three-evening praise and worship seminar attended by about 800 people. Many were set free in the area of praise and worship. God opened the doors to start a weekly power and light radio show with a 30-minute slot of contemporary Christian music.

Each December, Bonnie directs Christmas pageants that have grown in splendor, magnificence and power. A musical play written and directed by Bonnie had more than 350 in its cast and crew — including a 120-voice choir. The production was filmed by Zimbabwe Broadcasting Corporation and aired by popular demand. It is sought by many churches around the world and will be translated by a church in Kiev,

Ukraine, to be performed there.

Six years ago, Bonnie was invited to sing at a tea honoring the late wife of President Mugabe. There she sang the song she wrote for the Zimbabwe National Anthem competition and received a standing ovation. In 1994, Bonnie was invited to minister at an international ladies fellowship breakfast in Kampala, Uganda. She sang before 52 heads of state at the Organization of African Unity Summit. Most of Africa's leaders — Gadhafi, Arafat, Chiluba and Mandela — were in attendance, plus 200 ambassadors and world leaders.

In 1988, Tom reached out to Central Africa through an international conference in Harare's largest facility, which proved to be a wonderful vehicle. For 10 years, this conference has been held with over 5,000 people attending nightly last year, and seeing 800 new converts. Guest speakers included many internationally-known ministers.

Tom has taught the Word in Zambia, Malawi, Uganda, Tanzania, Kenya, Botswana and Mozambique. He teaches on accountability and breaking the bonds of iniquity.

Their new center now under construction in Harare will contain a 3,700-seat sanctuary with a 2,500 seat outdoor amphitheater and will house the Bible school, youth and college outreach facilities, day-care center and nursery, along with the children's church wing, bookshop, cafeteria and coffee shop. After years of prayer and negotiation, Tom was able to purchase acreage to begin these facilities.

In 1983, southern Africa was experiencing drought conditions, particularly in neighboring Mozambique, a war-torn country with no food and little water. The people were starving to death. Over a period of 10 years, Compassion

Ministries developed — out of the great need to help feed and clothe the 150,000 refugees who crossed into Zimbabwe. The refugees were repatriated to their home country in 1995; only then did Compassion Ministries see the fruit of their labor. Churches were established in the camps where more than 35,000 converts were discipled; this birthed a church planting revival in Mozambique. As a result, there are now village and city churches throughout western Mozambique receiving leadership training and discipleship.

To meet the needs of the poor and destitute, with the aftermath of the AIDS epidemic, Tom and Bonnie built an orphanage for 40 children. Another dormitory is under construction for 20 more AIDS victims.

Hardships over a decade of severe drought, fighting municipalities for their land, Marxist communism, racial prejudices, people fleeing the country in a mass exodus in search of a better social and economic situation, not to mention rampant inflation that keeps the country from progressing, yet by faith, Tom and Bonnie's commitment to build the church and the ministry with local support has held them in good stead. Their church has become one of the largest in the country, and they joyfully proclaim, "Surely, we have seen that God is Jehovah Jireh (our Provider)."

Chapter Nineteen

"Your Daughters Shall Prophesy"

A letter from Peggy Cooper Vilorio,
Tegucigalpa, Honduras:

I was born on Roatan, an island on the north coast of Honduras, a place called "a lost paradise." Though my life was not a bed of roses, God gave me beautiful Christian parents. Daddy was a sailor so we saw him only one month of the year. Therefore, Mother did her best to make two ends meet and raise God-fearing children. As children, we all participated actively in family chores; mine was that of selling bread and popcorn that Mother made at school.

Sundays were a holy day dedicated to the Lord. Going to church, memorizing God's Word, and resting from our work was the norm. I shall never forget the Sunday night when I was 12, my going to church passed from being a habit to having true meaning. After hearing the message, I ran to the altar recognizing that I had sinned and needed Jesus to save me. Ever since, Jesus has been real to me.

The following year, I left home to attend dorm school in

San Pedro Sula. This was the only way I could continue my schooling, as on Roatan there were no high schools. It was very difficult being away from my family. I remember lonely nights but feeling Jesus very close. Again, church was a ritual; every Sunday all 69 students lined up to walk to and from the services. Three years passed, during which I learned to survive, to wash and iron my clothes, and to make it on my own. I also learned to depend upon the Lord.

The next step was moving to the capital city in 1972 to continue my studies in a professional career. This brought many changes: a new living situation, new school, new friends, and a new church. I was satisfied knowing God; however, I had a sincere desire for more of Him. Then, someone spoke to me about the baptism in the Holy Spirit. As a good Baptist this was a "no no." I had been taught that this was from the devil, and I should not have anything to do with it; therefore, though I wanted more of God, I was fearful and doubtful regarding the issue.

As time passed, I continued seeking to know Him more, but I was so gripped by a spirit of fear and doubt, that I had to receive deliverance before I could receive the baptism in the Holy Spirit. What a difference this made in my life! One of the first things I remember was a hunger for God's Word and a deep desire to serve Him, and I did just that. Shortly after graduation, I landed a part-time job, and the rest of my time was dedicated to serving God in the ministry. I was excited!

One of the first responsibilities given me, was working with young ladies at a correctional center, where many came to know Jesus. In my effort to reach their families, I sought to find some of their parents; this was not accepted by the director of the center, and our permission to visit this place was cancelled. What had I done? I thought I was doing the right thing! But my pastor said I had done it all wrong, and thus, I was submitted to a discipline: that of not being able to serve at the center nor any other area. This being hard for me to understand, I decided to return to Roatan for a few weeks. I was disappointed, discouraged and confused.

Then one evening while I was sitting on a dock watching the sun go down, thinking to myself that if this was the result of serving God, I had had enough. While there, a missionary lady came by, and as if she knew all that was going through my mind, she began to speak prophetically of God's purpose for my life, and of His plan for me that was yet unfulfilled. Later on, she asked if I would be interested in becoming prepared to fulfill God's plan. She helped me get into Christian Retreat in Bradenton, Florida, where for 10 weeks I was enrolled in their course for "able ministers."

While there, my friend, Elizabeth, suggested I get in touch with Christ For The Nations Institute, and request a scholarship for foreign students. It all seemed so hard for a little island girl, who had sold bread to make a living. However, God put it together miraculously, and shortly thereafter, I found myself at CFNI, being prepared for things I did not know, but that God would have in my future.

It was a wonderful year; I learned the importance of prayer, and under Carroll Thompson's ministry, received inner healing and deliverance. I also learned to love serving God through the teachings of Ron Walrobe, Jim Hodges, Dr. Harold Reents, etc., and by working in the child evangelism department with Gwen Davis, and at headquarters, where I became personally acquainted with "Mom" Lindsay.

When it was time to return home, the door opened for a second-year scholarship at CFNI. I returned to Honduras to visit my family. Later, when I went to the U.S. Embassy for a visa to return to the U.S., the answer was "no." I knocked at every door I knew, and when none opened, I decided this was God's will for me: to stay in Honduras and serve Him.

I worked with youth on the island for a year before landing a job with an attractive salary, at a prestigious school in the capital city. One day God reminded me that I had been called — not to a secular job, but to serve Him. So I resigned my job and started serving at my church with the youth on a volunteer basis.

During this time, God again brought Mom Lindsay across my path, and I served as her translator during her visit to our nation's refugee camps, where CFN distributed relief goods. While at dinner one evening, she asked when I would be returning to CFNI to conclude my studies, and she reaffirmed that the door was still open. This was exciting! I then understood that four years earlier, when my visa was denied, God had not said, "no." He had just said, "Wait!"

So I returned to the U.S. Embassy and was easily given a visa to return to the U.S. to continue my second year at CFNI. This year was different, because I now had a new understanding of God and wanted to take full advantage of my time there. Upon conclusion, I happily returned to my country with a vision and a purpose: to be God's hand extended, reaching out to the oppressed.

Shortly after returning to Honduras, God gave me a very

special husband — Isaac Vilorio! While in preparation for our wedding, again Mom Lindsay visited Honduras, and while dining together, she handed me a generous gift toward my wedding dress. When our first baby arrived (we eventually had two: Christopher and Michael), "Gram" Lindsay made sure her gift was on the way. Far away, yet so close, so loving.

In Honduras, I became involved in full-time ministry, serving in the counseling ministry at our church. After 10 years, this has grown into a beautiful ministry with specialized counseling to couples, single mothers, youth, women, etc., including hospital visitation, and a prayer line that involves over 100 volunteer workers.

In December 1995, our pastor invited me to move from the counseling ministry to serve as an associate pastor at our church. Again, what a challenge! What did I know about being a pastor in a congregation of over 5,000 members, with a national and international outreach? Very little! But I learned that if I was willing, He would show me the way; and thus, I started a new odyssey with God, learning to hear His voice and depend totally on the Holy Spirit.

For Isaac and me, knowing and serving God has become the main purpose for living. As a civil engineer, Isaac has a secular job, and yet spends his afternoons as a volunteer, serving as director of the music ministry in our church.

Through the years, I have learned that to God, it does not matter who we are or what our background, He just requires our willingness to become channels of His Holy Spirit in order to fully use us. Therefore, when I find myself behind a pulpit speaking to thousands, or traveling to other cities or nations to share His Word, I am grateful that He chose me to be His servant, to bring Jesus' life, healing and deliverance to many. I will always be grateful for the inspiration and preparation I received at Christ For The Nations, as well as their continued support to me as a missionary on the field.

Part IV:
World
Changers
Network

Chapter Twenty

When Visions
Seem Too Big!

Gordon used to say, "If your life doesn't require a miracle every day, you're not living the way God wants you to live."

How would you feel if your team of evangelists paid their own way to go overseas to hold what turned out to be a mighty revival — with thousands attending, multitudes coming to Christ, many healed. Then after the revival crusade was over, the nationals and missionaries came to you with, "It would have been better if you had never come!"?

You'd be puzzled for the answer, wouldn't you? But that is exactly what happened!

"Why?," you're no doubt asking.

"Where will we put all these people to teach them, as our churches are few and very small? Without a solid foundation, many will return to their sinful ways, undoubtedly. And the Bible says, 'For everyone to whom much is given, from him much will be required' (Lk. 12:48). So now, since light has come to the people, if they don't walk in that light, they will be judged the more severely by the Lord. It would have been better if you hadn't come," was the pastors' response.

So Gordon and his team came back to the states troubled. They thought they had fulfilled their obligation of going into all the world to preach the Gospel, and now this: Build churches! But how? From where would the funds come? There was only one way to find out — pray. And that we did.

God's response was mystifying at first. It came just as we completed our annual Christ For The Nations convention, this time in Fair Park auditorium in Dallas. The hour was late when we crawled into bed on this final night, and we were quite weary. Soon both Gordon and I were sound asleep. Suddenly, I was awakened by what sounded like the ringing of an overseas phone call. (At that time there was a distinction between overseas and local rings.) I reached for the telephone, but realized the ringing was coming from my throat. What could it mean? Had I overworked? Was this the death rattle I had heard about, and was I getting ready to die? Then the ringing came from my ears. Puzzled, I lay there trying to figure it all out. Then the ringing moved to the top of my head. And I knew Gordon was hearing the sound, as every little bit he would stir and pull the covers further over his head.

"I won't wake him," I thought. "He needs his rest. But the first thing in the morning I'll ask him for an explanation." When the alarm went off a few hours later, I jumped out of bed. "What was I going to ask Gordon?" But I couldn't think of a thing, hard as I tried.

It was Sunday. That afternoon as Gordon and I were seated in our living room with an elderly lady, she began sharing with us some of her experiences. She told of a time God had spoken to her in a ringing.

The moment she spoke the word "ringing," my experience of the night before all came back to me. As I began to relate it, Gordon looked inquisitively at me, and said, "I heard all those rings. I thought it was the phone and wondered why you didn't answer it as you always did."

Then our guest, this little prophetess, began to speak, "God is calling you to build shelters, churches. The reason it sounded like a long distance call is that these churches are in other nations. You will go to those lands on occasion, speak to the people, hear their cries with your ears, and God will direct your mind as to how to accomplish all this."

Gordon and I looked at each other in amazement. How could we build churches — plural — when we didn't have the funds to build even one? We continued waiting on God as the days came and went.

Then one day, my niece and her husband, Rev. Herman and Viola Engelgau, who had been Assemblies of God missionaries in Upper Volta for many years, arrived on their first visit with us. As we sat at the dinner table, Herman said, "Oh, we have so many requests to help build churches; but when we apply to headquarters, our requests are usually denied. Often it takes most of their funds to support the workers. We could get the nationals to make the bricks and do the manual labor to build their churches, and if we had just $250, that would be enough to buy the items we can't make — like nails, cement, metal roofing and windows."

"That's the answer!" Gordon replied. (That was in 1961, before inflation, when money went much further.)

So in November that year, Gordon presented the Native

Church need in our monthly magazine, challenging donors to give $250 to sponsor a church, and at the same time, asking missionaries and nationals to state their need for a church, giving us references, etc. That first month's announcement brought 30 sponsors and 30 applications from overseas that met our criteria. This new arm of our missions' ministry was off to a good start!

By the time Gordon went to be with Jesus in 1973, we had helped build nearly 2,800 Native Churches. His death necessitated some big decisions.

What about the Native Church program? That was one way to lighten the financial load. "Discontinue it," my natural mind told me.

But as I began to write a letter to the nationals and missionaries with whom we were building Native Churches about our plans, the Lord spoke to my spirit: "Tell them that the program will continue. If you take that step of faith and trust me, I'll meet your other needs."

We did take that GIANT step of faith, and God has met us each step of the way.

If someone had told us that Gordon and I would be used to help build over 10,000 Native Churches in over 100 nations, we would no doubt have shaken our heads in disbelief. But as someone has said, "If the vision you have doesn't require God's intervention, then it's far too small."

To date, our donors have helped us build nearly 10,400 Native Churches. One of them was the first church Dr. Yonggi Cho of Seoul, Korea needed, which seated 1,000 people and is still being used today. His ministry has multiplied so greatly that he now has the world's largest congre-

gation — 750,000 members. Can you imagine what a sizeable reward our donors — who helped us build Cho's first
church — will have in heaven? Compounded interest!

Chapter Twenty-One

One of a Kind!

G ordon used to say, "Few ministers can stand the test of prosperity, popularity and power, and survive."

You are about to meet a man who did — not in the natural, carnal world, but in the spiritual, by God's standards. His name is Missionary Wayne Myers.

Who is this unassuming man who is respected and trusted the world over, who has prospered without a salary, who is "padre" (father) to thousands of ministers and missionaries (especially in Mexico), and who without promotion has faithfully served the Lord for 52 years in many nations?

Wayne was born in central Mississippi of humble parents. Even as a young boy he would read the Psalms and cry over them, though not understanding their full meaning. At age 14 in a little Baptist church, he surrendered his life to Jesus.

During World War II, Wayne enlisted in the Navy, where he was assigned to the U.S.S. Enterprise carrier in the South Pacific. On board the ship, he met "strange" sailors who worshiped a God whose dimension Wayne questioned. Every night, they prayed on the flight deck in the moonlight, and through the gifts of the Spirit, God revealed to them the ship would be hit, when and where it would take place, and how many people would die — several weeks before it happened! Wayne waited and watched, and when the attack took place exactly as the sailors said it would, Wayne declares, "It made a believer out of me."

But these sailors believed all sorts of "strange" things: They sang and worshiped God in an unknown language with such joy, praise and thanksgiving, Wayne kept his distance for a full year, watching some of them "slain in the Spirit." One night, he decided to go to the flight deck. To avoid what he observed was a violent contact with the deck, as some sailors were "slain in the Spirit," Wayne said he laid down flat on the deck. As some of the sailors gathered around him to pray with him (while others stood by mocking), Wayne said that for five solid hours the power of God flowed through him in ways he never dreamed of. "It was just like I'd latched on to 10,000 volts, which was the beginning of a brand new dimension of heaven for me, as I was baptized in the Holy Spirit," says Wayne.

After Wayne concluded his time in the Navy, he attended Bible college in Pasadena, California, where he spent from 4-15 hours daily, asking God to use his life. There, says Wayne, "The Lord spoke to me in a voice that was audible, 'I'm sending you to Mexico to bind my people together, not to build another faction in My body. Son, if you can learn at My feet, I can give you a crash course. Trust me for your health. Don't worry about the fact that you can't speak Spanish. I'll help you.'" (Wayne says he has ministered more in Spanish in the past years than in English, and his listeners often tell him he is more fluent in Spanish than in English.) "Then God said, 'As far as finances go, son, I own the cattle on a thousand hills and all the gold therein.' Then He repeated three times, 'Son, if you'll just give Me the glory, I'll use your life to bring many to a saving knowledge of My Son.' Later He impressed upon me this, 'I'm calling you to a faith walk, to totally trust Me. I won't permit you to share your personal needs with anybody, but with Me in prayer. Neither do I permit you to buy anything on credit, nor borrow 10 pennies from anybody. I must be the total Source and Sustainer of your life.'" Adds Wayne, "I'm not trying to establish an absolute for others, but this is how God led me."

Wayne did answer God's call to Mexico where he began by speaking to the children. He explained, "Children don't make fun of you when you make a mistake in speaking their language, so it helped me."

After being in the ministry five years, he met and married Martha, his faithful wife, a wonderful, constant helpmeet, and a godly influence on their three children and their grandchildren.

Wayne, who is known by his "living to give," "living just to serve," and "living just to bless" faith principles, has blessed millions in many nations, where these messages have rescued the listeners from a life of poverty and mediocrity to one of blessing and usefulness in God's Kingdom.

Brother Myers has worked closely with Christ For The Nations' Native Church program. In Mexico alone, he has supervised the building of 3,780 churches. Mega-churches are now being built in Mexico, where through Wayne and other nationals and missionaries whom he has led into the baptism in the Holy Spirit, they have caught his fire.

In other nations, he has equipped gospel workers with

bicycles, public address systems, jeeps, trucks, projectors, light plants, etc.

Wayne is a favorite speaker at Christ For The Nations Institute in Dallas, where he comes to speak each semester, as well as in our other 40 associated Bible schools. Many, many times, I personally have watched as he pulled out of his pocket a $20 or $50 bill to help some needy Christian worker. In fact, it seemed at times that he must have a mint in his pocket, since he never seemed to run out of cash — this in spite of the fact that he owns no home and his car is usually one that has been donated to him.

So is it any wonder that he is in demand as a speaker in conferences in Canada, Sweden, Australia, New Zealand, North and South America, Africa — and the whole world?

His three children and their families are all serving the Lord. David, who labored in Spain for 15 years, is presently on furlough. Rebecca and her husband, Greg Jacob are missionaries in Madrid, Spain — now for 20 years. Paula is married to a Christian physician.

A godly heritage for the next generation to follow, is the life and example of Wayne Myers!

Chapter Twenty-Two

Treasures in Heaven

Jesus said it: "Give to the poor, and you will have treasure in heaven" (Mk. 10:21).

When my husband, Gordon, died so suddenly from a heart attack on Sunday, April 1, 1973, on the platform of our partly-finished 1,400-seat auditorium, we had big financial challenges. (Later we enlarged the auditorium to seat 2,200.)

We had already borrowed $450,000 on the auditorium, and we needed another $300,000 to complete it. We had just bought seven neighboring apartment houses and a vacant bookstore; all except one had a 100 percent mortgage on them. It would take another three years to pay for our headquarters building. We had helped build 2,800 Native Churches overseas, and were committed to finish several more that were only half-completed. Besides all that, the day after Gordon died, we were $17,000 overdrawn at the bank! I knew we needed help. But where should we turn?

Shortly before Gordon's passing, as the two of us sat in our campus apartment living room, he said to me, "Call Norman." I asked, "Norman who?" He answered, "Norman Young that married your niece, Linda." My mind raced for a moment, wondering why the call. Then I replied, "If you are expecting Norm to come here to work at CFN, there isn't a ghost of a chance he'd come. He's vice president of a large bank in Portland, Oregon, is very active at the big Foursquare church, owns a number of apartment houses he has to oversee, and his parents are elderly. Linda's only sister lives there and her two little nieces are the apple of her eye, especially since she has no children of her own. She too is active in the church, is close to her parents, and has an excellent position as an executive secretary. There isn't a ghost of a chance they'd move here."

When I finished speaking, Gordon just softly said to me, "Call Norman." So being the obedient wife, I phoned Norm who happened to be home right then. When Gordon invited him to become our financial administrator, Norm repeated the very reasons I had already listed. But then he remarked, "In a couple of weeks, I have to make a trip to Fort Worth to look at some property on a lake the bank owns. I'll stop by."

Norm did spend that weekend with us, but flatly turned down Gordon's offer. Then Gordon responded, "If anything ever happened to me, Freda would need you." Whereupon, Norm slapped Gordon on the shoulder, saying, "Oh, you're going to be around for a long time. Aren't you?" Gordon's answer was, "Who can tell?" A few weeks later, Gordon was dead!

Gordon never did like to worry about "business." I recall when we were first married, he said to me, "I'm going to make you the financial director of our family. There's only one thing I require: Always keep us in the black!"

That may have sounded like a big task, but considering the amount of our income, the amazing thing was that we did stay in the black. We rarely borrowed — except for a car, a house, and a couple of times, for an appliance or a couch. I can hardly believe we made it when I now look at my diary of those early years and see that we would receive often less than $3 a week in our evangelistic meetings.

But as our ministry grew, I did in fact guide the income, keep the bills paid, and usually negotiated on any large purchases the ministry needed. Gordon was busy writing 250 books, preaching in conferences at home and abroad.

Norman and Linda came for Gordon's funeral, but felt they just couldn't make a move to Dallas, even though I reminded Norm of Gordon's conversation. So for about a year I struggled on, the Lord helping me, as we paid off the headquarters and kept all accounts current. My daughter, Shira, miraculously returning from Israel two days before her dad died, said to me, "Mom, surround yourself with employees smarter than you are in special areas. You can't know all the answers, and don't expect those carrying the business end of this ministry to be in fasting and prayer all day. They'll have their work to do." Good advice. I kept thinking and praying about Norm and Linda.

One year later, Norm and Linda decided to move to Dallas, much to my relief. So Norm, Leo Cornelius, our chief accountant at CFN, and I shoved things into high gear. For the next 14 years, we built more overseas Native Churches, bought another adjoining apartment as our Bible school and work grew, printed more gospel literature, started several foreign Bible schools, built our Student Center, the Library Chapel, and Cornerstone complex, and secured and paid for the 10-story Sheraton for our men's dorm and school cafeteria. The ministry and magnitude of Christ For The Nations Institute more than quadrupled in size — for which we continually praise God.

Norm and Linda traveled the world with me over those 14 years as we visited the various outreaches of this ministry. We saw millions of people — many half-starved and poorly clothed, especially the children — that greatly moved our hearts. Upon our return to Dallas, Norm made contacts to secure surplus food, clothing and medical supplies to ship to the needy, and we raised the funds for the freight. But it was on a small scale.

After 14 years, Norm and Linda left us with many tears, to return to Portland. But by now, we were solvent at CFN — every campus building was paid for.

Norm and Linda couldn't forget the many needy souls they had met in our travels so they sought the Lord for the next step of their lives. The nations were calling for help, while at the same time, U.S. corporations were contacting them to offer all sorts of supplies — food, clothing, blankets, and medical provisions — some of them taking tax write-offs. Since CFN did not now have anyone on staff to continue the relief efforts Norm had started while employed in Dallas, we tied in with him as he organized the nonprofit Global Assistance program, which has been greatly blessed of the Lord. I asked Norman to give me an update of our joint efforts, just before we go to press on this new book. Here is the report he sent me:

"One of the most gratifying experiences we have had over the years is to provide material assistance to people who are suffering from famine, war or other disasters and, in many cases, whose very lives have been threatened.

"We have been involved in supplying food, clothing and medical supplies to the 'boat people' of Cambodia; to the victims of the Mexico City earthquake; to the victims of the famine and war in Southern Chad and Sudan; to the war-ravaged Indians on the Honduran/Nicaraguan border; and to many other countries where lives are in peril.

"It is impossible to stand in front of a hungry man and only offer him a tract. Anyone in this position has to reach out to the hurting with food, clothing or medical supplies that will meet his immediate need.

"We have shipped approximately 600 8 feet by 20 feet or 8 feet by 40 feet ocean containers to various parts of the world, with our focus being on the former Soviet Union. Four hundred containers alone have been shipped to that vast area, mostly to Belarus, Moldova, Russia and the Ukraine.

"By reaching out to these people, we have seen Christian works given freedom and actually advanced by those formerly communist leaders who have melted as a result of the compassion and concern shown.

"We have warehouse space near Baltimore, Maryland, and space available in Dallas, Texas. Our registration with USAID has provided us with freight funding and access to military surplus property for select projects.

"In the winter of 1991, we visited Moscow and Minsk after having shipped several ocean containers of humanitarian aid to those two areas. In Minsk, we met with city officials, church leaders, and the Belarussian Children's Fund (BCF). As a result, we now are in our eighth year of partnering with BCF and others. We have established a child sponsorship program for children at risk in and around Minsk; have provided medical supplies to the hospitals treating people effected by the Chernobyl accident; supplied food and clothing to the elderly and poor who have been ravaged by the effects of sky-rocketing inflation over the last decade — inflation so bad that in 1990, 50,000 rubles would purchase five automobiles and now in 1999, it will purchase two loaves of bread. A pensioner in Belarus has less than $10 per month on which to live in a society where food prices are very near those we pay in the West.

"We have shipped a fully-equipped ambulance to Minsk, Belarus; a school bus to Honduras; have organized a large tent crusade in Romania; provided cancer-fighting drugs to the Ukraine and Belarus; provided a field hospital to Central America; sent medical teams to Belarus and Honduras; helped organize evangelistic rallies in Nepal, Honduras, Belarus, Romania and Russia, along with providing 600 containers of humanitarian aid worth approximately $60 million. This is far more assistance than our initial dream could even have realized or imagined.

"The assistance we have sent around the world has made a difference in thousands of lives and is nothing less than what we are instructed to do in the Scripture."

> He who gives to the poor will not lack, but he who hides his eyes will have many curses (Prov. 28:27).

> Pure and undefiled religion before God and the Father is this: to visit orphans and widows in their trouble, *and* to keep oneself unspotted from the world (Jas. 1:27).

Part V:
A Family
of World
Changers

Chapter Twenty-Three

To the Jew First

From Shira Lindsay Sorko-Ram

As far back as I can remember, my father had a deep love for the Jewish people and an equally deep longing to see them come into their full destiny in God. As an 8-year-old child in a small town high in the mountains of Northwest America, I recall my folk listening to the radio and hearing the report that Israel had just become a state. Jews from all over the world were streaming back to the ancient land of Israel. I asked my dad what was making them do that, and he answered, "God, Himself, is bringing them back to their home."

Growing up, I remember the continuous prayers of my family for Israel and the faith that my parents had that God was going to save the Jewish people and return them to Himself. And that became ingrained in the fabric of who I am.

Then in my teenage years, I walked away far from God and all spiritual things, including the prophetic future of Israel. But slowly as God began to draw me back to Him, the seed that had been planted in me concerning Israel began to grow. Still I had no desire to live in Israel, nor did I see myself as destined to become a part of the Jewish people. Nevertheless, I decided to go with my parents on a tour to Israel in 1967, right after the Six Day War. Jerusalem had just been reunited into one city under Israel's sovereignty. One could not deny that God was again visibly moving on behalf of the Jewish people.

Through a set of God-directed events, I became a Jew and an Israeli citizen, as I closely identified with the people to whom God had sent me. Interestingly enough, years later, my mother revealed that she was quite certain that her own maternal grandmother had been a Jewess from the Soviet Union. My destiny was unfolding.

In 1976, I returned to the United States for a visit. There were so few Israeli believers that I felt the most important thing I could do was to make a call to the Jewish believers in America to "come home." If the Bible said that God would bring His chosen people back to the land of Israel in the last days, it only made sense that Bible-believing Jews would and should receive that great promise.

At that time, I met Ari Sorko-Ram, an actor in Hollywood. A mutual friend told me about him. "You need to meet Ari," he said. "He is a born-again Jew and has talked about immigrating some day to Israel." That attracted my attention, because the main purpose for my trip to the states had been to beat the bushes for believing Jews who would catch the vision to move to Israel and become a light to our people.

Within three months, Ari had left his Hollywood career and moved to Israel. He had given the Lord a list of things that would have to be worked out for him to come to Israel, including being released from a new television series for which he had just contracted. To his amazement, within weeks, all had fallen into place.

Six months later, we were married. Together we began to conduct Bible classes, and by 1980, we had the beginnings of a new congregation in the coastal town of Netanya. Along with that, we were blessed with two children: a son, Ayal, and a daughter, Shani — both of whom are native-born Israelis and are equally fluent in both Hebrew and English. We and our congregation then moved to Tel Aviv, and for eight years, we pastored and raised our children. By 1988, we had a congregation of about 100 people, including immigrants from America, Europe and a few native-born Israelis.

During this time, we became aware that our son had a serious learning disability. He was diagnosed as dyslexic and hyperactive. We agonized in prayer over him, but saw no improvement. Finally in 1988, we made a decision to move to Dallas, Texas, for two years to give him opportunity for special schooling that was not available in Israel. We left the congregation in the hands of two elders.

Ayal made great progress the first year in special education. The second year, because of the cost and other factors, we decided to homeschool both children. This allowed us to travel and speak in congregations across America. It was a wonderful time for us and our children as we visited many states, spoke in meetings and homeschooled the kids. Ayal made tremendous progress, moving from first to fifth grade level in those two years.

One day when we were traveling in California, Ayal, who had severe memory problems, began to respond to questions in his school courses that made us know he had received a phenomenal healing. Today, Ayal has a brilliant mind and is working with us in setting up our computer programs and our video and sound equipment for our new facility.

At the same time our son received his healing, to our dismay, we received word that the congregation we had left with our elders was collapsing. There was much rancor and division within the congregation, with accusations flying back and forth as to the cause of the collapse — some of the accusations pointed at us, even though we were in the U.S. when it happened.

When we first received word of the trouble that was brewing, we contemplated cutting our time in the U.S. short in order to return in an attempt to save the congregation. However, we knew that our son would not be able to get the care he was receiving and, indeed, needed if we went back to Israel. And so, from afar we watched our congregation disintegrate. We were brokenhearted! We felt as if we had lost a child. Close to 10 years of our work was slipping down the drain.

Looking back, we realize that God did an enormous work in our own lives during those two years. He refined us, cutting off a lot of rough edges, and gave us much new wisdom in dealing with the sheep of our flock and with other leaders.

Ari and I are pioneer types, breaking through walls, pushing through to new frontiers of faith, and believing God for the impossible — important elements for working in Israel. But through this sorrowful time with our congregation, we softened. God put in us the spirit of a "mom and pop" to our sheep. Today, we are thankful for that trial.

We returned to Israel and for five years, worked on projects that were more nationally oriented. We sponsored several National Israeli Messianic Leadership Conferences, published Hebrew translations of a number of books, and built strong relations with Messianic leaders throughout the land. To provide enough funds to live on, Ari worked on another television series of which a part was filmed in Israel and part in South Africa.

Even though our son was doing well, our daughter, Shani (who was 14 years old at the time), began to show severe signs of alienation from us. Her rebellion deepened until we were not able to cope with the situation. We cried out to God, and He intervened by opening a door for us to send her to a godly home for troubled teenagers. After 18 months in that Texas home, Shani had found herself and returned to God and her family.

Since her high school days, she has been earning money as a photographer, and she is a great humorous writer, as well. At this writing, she is completing the final months of Bible school and planning for her marriage. Both she and her fiance are gifted musicians who plan to reside in Israel and join our work there. Also our son, Ayal, is working with us full time in the ministry. What a tribute to the faithfulness of a loving and merciful God!

In 1994, we felt the time had come to do some public street witnessing. Through drama, song and mime, we attracted large crowds. When we invited them to come to a Bible bookstore for further talk about the Messiah, we had far more people than we could accommodate. And we had no way to follow up in discipleship classes with such large numbers of seekers. Out of that street ministry came the next step for our lives. We knew that it was time to raise up another congregation — one of evangelists, disciples and leaders that could multiply themselves many times over. We knew that was the only way we could attempt to realize the vision God had planted deep within us. We could never meet the demands of all these hungry souls by ourselves.

In 1995, we began a new Messianic Jewish congregation in the Tel Aviv area, and we felt our hearts focusing on a very specific challenge: We wanted to reach the Sabras of Israel. A Sabra is a native-born Israeli, as opposed to Jews who immigrated to Israel from other lands. To accomplish this purpose, we set out with three goals or purposes in mind: to be a Messianic Jewish congregation that ministered to Israelis by functioning only in the Hebrew language, to communicate that they did not have to surrender their heritage and traditions; and to be full of the love and power of Yeshua through the Holy Spirit.

Until very recently, most born-again Israelis had originally immigrated from other nations, such as America, Europe, Russia or Ethiopia. Out of approximately 7,000 Israeli believers today, only about 1,000 are Sabras. We felt compelled to reach out specifically to those Israelis who were born and raised in Israel. That meant we would conduct our meetings only in Hebrew with no translations into other languages. This was uncommon among congregations in Israel, as most were primarily made up of immigrants with a variety of mother tongues.

Secondly, we felt strongly that the Israeli people needed

to know that to believe in Yeshua did not entail having to leave their Jewish heritage. The opposite! Believing in Yeshua should cause an Israeli to be even more Jewish! After all, Yeshua (Jesus) Himself was born and raised Jewish, and in the Scriptures, He is called the King of the Jews and the Lion of Judah. The majority of Israelis don't even believe in God, let alone the Messiah. Understandably then, it would be nearly impossible to comprehend the purpose of being a chosen nation — a purpose which the prophets identify as being a light to the nations.

We are convinced from the Scripture that God has a purpose for Israel which has not yet been fulfilled in its entirety. Paul said that the gifts and callings of God are without repentance — meaning irrevocable. And the prophets interpreted that call to be a light to the nations (Isa. 60). Zechariah said the day will come when 10 men will take hold of the garment of a Jew and say, "We're going with you, because we have heard that God is with you." Therefore, our congregation had to be a congregation of believing Jews within the framework of Messianic Judaism.

Thirdly, our congregation must operate in the love and power of Yeshua through the Holy Spirit. Israelis have absolutely no interest in any religion that professes a form of godliness without also having the power of a living, intimately-involved God. Therefore, we must preach and practice a living Gospel in which lives are actually renewed, bodies are actually healed, and circumstances are miraculously changed. Theory will never be enough for Israelis. Our belief system has to work.

This then is the plan we have followed, and today we have

a growing Messianic Jewish congregation of Sabra Israelis whose lives have been transformed by Yeshua. They are full of the Holy Spirit and boldly reaching out to their families, friends and business acquaintances in the Tel Aviv area.

In 1997, we felt God was speaking to us with new urgency. His message to our hearts was this: "You have prayed for revival in Israel for many years; now prepare for it, for revival is at hand." He then spoke to us that we were to prepare in three very specific ways:

Acquire a larger facility. We must have a larger barn for the harvest, larger nets for the fish that will be coming to the Master.

Translate into Hebrew and publish as many Spirit-filled books with the foundational truths of the Scripture as possible. Once the expensive process of translating and publishing a book is done, we are then able to reach 10 people, 100, 1,000, or 50,000 with these fundamental truths. In order that the revival can allow for godly discipling, we must have materials ready. This vision has expanded now to include video and audio materials. Videos can be subtitled in Hebrew, and we can distribute teachings on audiotape that have been originally preached in Hebrew. All of these are valuable tools for the coming revival.

The third instruction that came to us from the Holy Spirit was to train national leaders. The coming revival must have Israeli leadership. The possibility of doing this is coming to pass as we move into a cell congregation. We are working toward the goal that, within nine months to a year, we will be able to bring Israelis from a state of no knowledge of the Scriptures or of God to where they have a foundational knowledge of the Word of God; their lives have been changed and their minds renewed to a degree that they are able to begin reproducing the life of Yeshua through cell meetings in their own homes.

These goals are the focus of our lives, and we intend to fulfill our days doing this until Yeshua comes back to earth or we join Him in heaven.

In the last few years, religious persecution has increased significantly in Israel. As the government system of parliamentary coalition becomes more fractured and increasingly inoperable, ultra-Orthodox politicians are able to sell their pivotal votes to the highest bidder among the major ruling political parties. They are thus able to extract funds, create laws and impose their will on Israel's body politic far beyond what their members would naturally generate. At the same time, the secular population of Israel is becoming more and more rudderless, without goals, without leadership and without hope. In this situation, the Orthodox are able to impose their agenda.

And they are fanatical, full of hatred and suspicion against all other belief and value systems, including the reform and conservative branches of Judaism. They are extremely focused on their own agenda. When elections come up, nearly all ultra-Orthodox vote according to the instructions of their rabbis. Therefore, even though the Orthodox represent only 20 percent of the population, they are a force which wields enormous power in the Knesset (Israel's parliament). And they are enormously threatened by the growing presence of the Messianic Jews whom they rightly perceive to be a committed group of people with a faith that does not pay allegiance to rabbinical leadership.

The stated goal of the Orthodox political leadership is to impose a theocratic government on the Israeli people. Their dream is to replace Israel's legal system with rabbinical law accompanied with rabbinical punishment. They view democracy as an enemy of rabbinic Judaism, much as fanatical Muslim forces see democracy as an enemy of Islam.

Israelis face two devastating fronts of conflict as the new century begins: the Israeli-Arab conflict and the secular-religious conflict. Many intellectuals and journalists feel that this second conflict is even more serious and deadly than the first.

Notwithstanding this setting, the Messianic movement in Israel has suddenly begun to rapidly expand. Israelis, who fear for the continued existence of the state of Israel, are desperately looking for spiritual help.

Messianic congregations do not have access to radio or television and are generally harassed by ultra-Orthodox elements. Nevertheless, Israelis are coming into contact with believers in the land, and when they hear the truth, many are accepting the Messiah as their Savior and Israel's only hope.

Even as the power of the ultra-Orthodox grows, the numbers of born-again believers are increasing, and we are receiving more and more media attention. Even 15 years ago, most Israelis had never heard of Messianic Jews. Today, most have.

And today the Messianic believers of Israel are becoming increasingly strong and bold. If the ultra-Orthodox ever do succeed in passing legislation to outlaw sharing our faith in Yeshua, many Israeli believers would be ready to go to prison. We feel that it would be foolish of Satan to enact such a law, because if and when an Israeli is jailed for his faith in

Yeshua, it will bring our movement to the forefront of media coverage as nothing ever has in the last 18 centuries.

It is this atmosphere in which we live and work for the God of our salvation. With the eyes of our hearts we already see tens of thousands of Israelis coming to the Lord. Then everything we have gone through these last 30 years will have been worth it. Perhaps that is one reason that God has put in His Word so many times — both Old and New Testaments — that He is going to save all Israel. He has recorded these promises so that no matter how hopeless the situation looks, how stiff-necked our people, and how blinded the religious leaders, all Israel shall be saved! Israel's call and gifts are without repentance. Israel will fulfill its calling as expressed by the ancient prophet, Isaiah:

> Arise, shine; for your light has come! And the glory of the LORD is risen upon you. For behold, the darkness shall cover the earth, and deep darkness the people; but the LORD will arise over you, and His glory will be seen upon you. The Gentiles shall come to your light, and kings to the brightness of your rising (Isa. 60:1-3).

> But you shall be named the priests of the LORD, they shall call you the servants of our God. You shall eat the riches of the Gentiles, and in their glory you shall boast (Isa. 61:6).

Why should God allow our family to live and work in Israel at such a time as this when history is drawing to a close and prophecy moves toward its final realization? I don't know, but I cannot think of a greater honor than having a part in seeing Israel, prodigal Israel, return to the arms of the Father.

Chapter Twenty-Four

Against Impossible Odds — But God

Gilbert Lindsay Story

The Lord gave the word: great *was* the company
of those that published *it* (Psa. 68:11 KJV).

On a Tuesday night in November 1990, I boarded a plane
for Moscow. From the natural, it made no sense, therefore, I did not tell my mom or my brother that I was going.
Only my wife, Shirley, and my children knew.

Why was I going? I had heard there was a possibility of
doing some Christian printing in Minsk, Belarus. Even
though I had been in printing all my life, I knew no one who
needed Russian books, nor did I know how to do business in
a foreign country.

The next evening, my wife went to church. A lady I did
not know gave Shirley a two-page letter which she said God
woke her up to write. She wrote these things down about the
same time I was landing in Moscow.

The letter said that God had prepared me all my life for
what was about to happen. God was sending me overseas in

a venture that was beyond my dreams, and I was not to worry because God would protect me.

Arriving at the Moscow Airport for the first time was not necessarily a good dream. I boarded a train and traveled overnight to Minsk. At this time, it was about the only way to get there. Even though Minsk has 1,700,000 people, it had no contact with the outside world. No Western airlines went there at all.

Of the many shocks I received on my first trip to Minsk, one was greater than the others. All the stores were bare, except for the hard currency stores — ones where you can pay only in dollars. I had always heard how the Soviet people were so proud of their country. Now I was in the Soviet Union and I saw stores that did not want Russian rubles. Why? Could I imagine a store in Dallas accepting Russian rubles only? This was just the beginning of my education of the poor economy of the U.S.S.R.

When I arrived back in Dallas, my first call was to Chaplain Ray of International Prison Ministries to see if he needed any printing done in the U.S.S.R. He said, "Yes, I need 50,000 New Testaments" — my first Russian job. At this time, I did not have even a glimpse of what was going to take place. In January, 1991, I printed Kenneth Hagin books, 1,000,000 New Testaments for Terry Law Ministries, and another 1,000,000 for International Bible Society.

I had no equipment in Minsk, so I had to use the Russian printing plants, which were at 100 percent capacity printing local and communist literature. One plant made a deal with me to print 2,000,000 New Testaments in four months. I went to Minsk once a month for the first year trying to get the job done. By the end of the year, that printing plant had printed only 300,000 of the 2,000,000 order.

Another problem was getting paper. One plant said they would print the job, but had no paper. We went to the paper mill; they would make paper for us, but they had no pulp. We went to the pulp mill; they would make pulp, but they had no wood. We then went to foresters, bought them saws to provide wood, and promised them two trucks of meat from Minsk. The meat was delivered, and the whole chain seemed to work, ever so slowly.

By the first summer, I had received an order of 100,000 Bibles for Matt Tutor of Family Radio. The printing plant kept me updated on the proof, printing and binding. In June, Matt met me in Minsk to view the job at the Communist Printing Plant. To my surprise, the plant would not let us in the first, second or third day. I sent someone else to check on the job. The reason they wouldn't let us in was because they had never started the job, and just made up the process and information they were sending me. Times were tough, to put it very simply.

By August, the Bibles were printed and waiting for binding. The Communist Printing Plant had printed them, but did not want to bind them, because when they were bound they would look like Bibles. This might get them in trouble with their communist bosses.

On a Monday morning, I went to the Communist Printing Plant. Shirley, at the hotel, went down for breakfast. An American came into the restaurant, said that Gorbachev had just been killed and they were getting out of the country instantly. My wife did not know how to get in touch with me, so she decided she might just as well enjoy breakfast.

Back at the plant, I could see no one. All the bosses were in a meeting. A coup had just taken place in Moscow, and the Russians did not know who their leader was. If they chose the wrong leader and he was ousted, they would lose their jobs and probably go to jail.

My wife and I had already planned to go to Moscow by train on Monday night. Now that the coup was in progress, should we risk it? We went anyway. On Tuesday morning, we arrived in Moscow and saw the tanks lining the streets. Being an optimist, I didn't think things looked too serious, and only later when I read the report in *Time*, did I realize how serious the situation was.

Tuesday, we had two appointments in our search for additional help in printing the 2,000,000 New Testaments that was going so slowly. The first man we met was a friend of Boris Yeltsin. At this time Boris Yeltsin was in his "White House," surrounded by a mob of people protecting him from the men who started the coup. Boris called this friend and asked him to print 1,000,000 flyers by that evening for distribution in the subway.

Our next meeting was with Paul Posner, brother of Vladimir Posner, who was the spokesman of the U.S.S.R. to the West. I had seen Vladimir many times on television and could not believe that I was meeting with his brother. After the meetings, Shirley and I returned to Minsk. Besides seeing the tanks, the only thing that was unusual in Moscow was that McDonalds did not have the normal one-hour waiting line.

Through these and other contacts we were able to get most

of the original 2,000,000 New Testaments printed. The Communist Printing Plant finally shipped the 100,000 Bibles to another printing plant for binding, so they would not get in trouble.

On one occasion, I had received a very good price on printing a four-color booklet, *The Story of Jesus*. The printing plant had used imported paper for the job, and the cost was just a little more than the price of the paper from the West. How they could do this? I went to the deputy director of this printing plant some months later and asked him. Without blinking an eye, he said, "It is simple. I stole the paper." What do you do or say?

At the very beginning, I worked a joint venture — I was to bring the jobs; they were to handle the printing. Unfortunately, I had to go every month and check on my jobs. In March 1991, the main interpreter and coordinator of my jobs went on a business trip to the United States.

The joint venture sent Olga Yushkevich, a lady from a labor pool, who would work only one or two days. I gave her a job with many details for Chaplain Ray, and was amazed at her ability for details. The joint venture hired her. She was very talented, and had graduated valedictorian of her high school class, and at the top of the Institute of Linguistics in Minsk. Even with these credentials, she was earning only $4 a month and barely existed by teaching English to Jewish immigrants planning a move to the United States. Even though the joint venture had about 15 people working on my jobs, Olga was the only one that could answer any question. Because of her diligence and honesty, my customers came to love her, which made the people in the joint venture mad.

She was not allowed to fax me, nor was she given a desk to handle a million dollars worth of Christian printing.

Later that year, I decided to put in my own printing plant. At this time there were virtually no western manufacturing companies in the U.S.S.R. The coup was over, and Gorbachev had won. Things seemed to be "normal." I started sending printing equipment to Minsk: a web press, a four-color sheet-fed press, and all kinds of bindery equipment. But where was I to put it? There were no buildings for sale and even if there were, a foreigner could not buy a building.

Our office was in the Planeta Hotel, where we had a suite on the 11th floor and four offices on the 12th floor. One day I received a call stating that the KGB wanted to meet with me at my office in Minsk. They came to the point very quickly: They had heard that I wanted to put in a printing plant. "Yes." Would I consider putting my printing plant in their new building? They had just moved into a new five-story building; the bottom two floors were empty and available. I asked them if they knew that I printed Bibles. "Yes, and that is not a problem." They took me to the head of the Belarussian KGB that day, and he confirmed the offer. I also told them we might put in a Bible school. In that case, they could even move out of the building totally and go back to their old building! We then took our friends at the Communist Printing Plant to see the KGB building, but it was not suitable.

After looking everywhere, we finally found a building owned by the Academy of Science (AOS). It housed their printing plant, but they used only a small part of the building. We moved our equipment into about 50,000 square feet of space.

It was a great feeling to have control of what job to print next. Our equipment was quite capable of printing huge jobs. We could print a railroad car of paper every day. But there were more challenges. Many, many more.

It was incredible seeing the people with their new-found freedom, hunger for Christ. Christian Broadcasting Network, Pat Robertson's organization, contacted me. They had gone on television in Russia and were receiving millions of responses by mail. We printed for CBN over 10,000,000 booklets for youth and adults during a short period of time.

The man I originally hired as general director, negotiated a poor contract, and within a short time, I was paying $16,000 a month for rent, which is much more than the cost in Dallas. To make things worse, the AOS printing plant managers looked at us as the enemy. Even though the AOS paid them only about $20 a month, they thought they should charge $27,000 a month for rent. Every month when I paid my rent, they would turn off the power to my equipment. To this day, they have offered no explanation.

Because of these and other problems, I promoted Olga Yushkevich to general director of the entire plant. As deputy director, she had really been the brains of the company. By now, we had several quality printing managers, and Olga showed that she could pull things together.

In January 1994, our son, Michael, came to work with us. The previous year, he had worked in the computer department of a local store. The experience had trained him to handle all of our computer problems. With 50,000 square feet of printing equipment, many supplies and parts are required.

Since the presses and bindery equipment are from the West, all the parts have to be bought from the West. Michael oversees this very important job, making at least one air shipment of parts every week.

Even though the top people in the Academy of Science were our friends, the people beneath them made life impossible. Soviet laws made the lower bosses independent from the upper bosses. The first crisis came one Friday evening in October 1994, when the AOS printing plant called the militia and took our customers out at gunpoint, locking all our workers out of the building. By Monday morning, we were in touch with the AOS bosses downtown, who allowed us back in the building.

The problems came so often that Olga, my director, filed a lawsuit in the top court in Belarus. In January 1995, our case was heard by the Justice of the Supreme Court of Belarus. The court helped us beyond our expectations. They ruled that the maximum they could charge us for rent was $7,000 a month. Praise the Lord, this was a real answer to prayer.

In February, the head of the AOS printing plant told our workers they were closing our company permanently in about two weeks. Our workers did not know whom to believe. The AOS was a powerful organization, so why should they not believe them?

All this time, the AOS printing plant made no demands of any kind; just that they were going to close us down. We again contacted the AOS downtown. They fired the heads of their printing plant, and allowed us to put our man as the head of their printing plant. Unfortunately, the fired bosses did not accept the firing, and on the given date, turned off the power and left the building. It took us two days to get the power back on. Our man did, however, become the boss of their plant, but the fired bosses got their jobs back after appealing to the President's Commission.

By now another problem had developed. An ex-employee had bribed a tax man; they sent three investigators to our company, spending three months full time investigating us. They demanded $36,000 in March, which I paid. In April, they demanded another $30,000, which I refused to pay.

By May, the old bosses of the AOS had threatened the new boss, so he took sick leave and left. This left the old bosses back in control. They told me that on May 17, 1995, they would close us permanently.

I decided to go the American Embassy and ask for help, and was met by Tamara Fitzgerald, who asked if I was Gordon Lindsay. I said, "No, why?" She did not know. Later in the meeting, I asked her again "Why Gordon Lindsay?" She said, "Didn't he write a lot of Christian books?" I answered, "Yes, and he was my father." She then told me she was a Christian, and was going to help us.

My staff contacted the chairman of the committee of foreign affairs in parliament for Belarus. He agreed that what the tax people were doing was illegal, as were the activities of the Academy of Science Printing Plant.

By the end of April, Olga told me that the threats were just too much, and she was unsure if she would stay. Several days later, at Trinity Church in Cedar Hill, Texas, where we attend regularly, I met Arkady Silvanovich for the second time. He was there with a friend and was one of the associate pastors of a church in Belarus. I asked him if he would consider becoming my general director. Arkady had been a part of the underground church for many years and was highly educated. He accepted.

I will never forget that Friday, May 19, 1995. The AOS Printing Plant managers again turned off the power to my equipment and locked our workers out of the building. They came and tore the telephone out of the wall while I was there. On Monday, our workers returned to work but were not allowed in the offices or shop area. To make matters worse, the tax man approached our workers and said that Gilbert Lindsay was a criminal, and his department was going to close me down. I now had two critical problems. There was nothing left but prayer and perseverance. It looked impossible.

To our dismay, our friend in parliament was in a runoff election and was not expected to win. He was in no position to help us.

The whole week was agony, beyond imagination. Jobs, cash flow, and answers were at a standstill. The tax people had closed our bank account and refused to let us pay our workers. Arkady and I spent the whole week between the tax office and the Academy of Science headquarters. The tax people would not see me. The president of the Academy of Science was on our side, but had lost total control of the plant. He wanted to fire his workers again but because of their contacts with the President's Commission, he could not. We accomplished absolutely nothing the whole week and our workers were beginning to wonder if we had a company.

During this week, Olga's apartment was set on fire, and

she could not handle it anymore. Several weeks later, I offered Olga a job in Dallas. She had a world of knowledge and our customers had grown to depend on her.

It would have been easier to quit than to keep going. I told everyone that we would survive because God was on our side, and we had no other option.

On Sunday, Shirley and I went to the International Church in Minsk, where we asked for prayer that our friend in parliament, Mr. Tereshko, would win re-election that day. The next day, we learned he had won. Arkady and I went immediately to his office and told him that we believed God had a purpose in his winning. He agreed with us and pledged to help us. We spent most of the whole week in his office. During the week, he called the president of the AOS and the tax man many times, and also got the prosecutor's office involved in trying to help the AOS remove the heads of the AOS printing plant.

On Friday, I received a call from Mr. Tereshko who arranged a meeting with the assistant to the president of the country. They were sending out the special forces, militia, and prosecutor's office to open up our plant. The AOS personnel blocking our equipment were removed, and shortly afterwards, were fired. Within several months, the AOS shut down their plant completely, which was about the best news I could have received. Even with the shutdown, most of our customers never noticed any problem in deliveries.

Finally, Arkady and I were permitted to talk with the top tax man in Belarus. He yelled at me for a solid hour; in his mind, I was the reason that his farmers had not been paid for two months. He vowed to send more men to try to find more taxes he could collect from us. We were allowed to operate again, but the future was still cloudy at this time.

By the first of July, the tax people demanded $700,000 cash, but we kept on printing. About that time, Tamara Fitzgerald told me to call the U.S. Commerce Department. They were expecting my phone call. I was informed that the minister of economy of Belarus, Mr. Baday, was flying to Washington for a meeting. They told me to write my problems on two pages, but they would not be able to discuss my problems as it was a high level meeting. Two days later, they called me back. The only thing they talked about in the meeting was our problem — if Belarus could not work with me, they could work with no one. I was instructed to fly to Minsk immediately and meet with Mr. Baday, which I did. He listened to my problems and offered to help. He initiated a new committee of three legal assistants; we met with our attorneys and these three lawyers. Within a day, we had the full support of these three departments.

In August, the President's Commission sued us, saying we had harmed the AOS directors who were fired. The government wanted $78,000 from us, even though it was the AOS, along with parliament and the prosecutors who had them fired. With God's help we won, and the directors did not get their jobs back.

Also that month, we approached Mr. Tereshko from parliament and asked him to give us a ruling on whether the law passed by parliament was legal, and if it protected us from the tax people. We knew the law did, but we wanted an official statement. Mr. Tereshko did not want to go out on a political limb, so he gathered all the top legal people in the country and invited our attorney to the meeting. In the meeting, we had the support of everyone except the tax man, who said, "Why do we have such a stupid law since we don't pay any attention to it?"

Finally in November 1995, we went to the Supreme Court of Belarus and all the top government people witnessed in our behalf against the tax department. After a year and a half, it was over; we had won, and the $700,000 tax was dismissed as illegal.

We still had one last court case pending. The AOS printing plant lawyers still sued us for $49,000 back rent and $50,000 in late penalties. We had subtracted this rent due to all the continuing problems, taking into account the time that we were unable to print. We had done this for survival. In defense, we sued them for $111,000 in damages. According to Soviet law, we were to pay them no matter what they had done. Our only defense was to go for damages to negate their suit. Again, miraculously, the Supreme Court awarded them $99,000 and awarded us $111,000.

In January 1997, Arkady left the company to resume his place as associate pastor of a church in Minsk. The congregation is presently building a church — one of the few churches being built in the former Soviet Union. Previously, the church had moved into a tent to help save the $500 a month for rent. Since they had no heat during the bitterly cold, Belarussian winter, they set up a saw mill on their property, bought trees, and made their own lumber. Half of the building has been completed; the walls are up on the main auditorium. However, they do not have the $20,000 for the roof; it will take a miracle from God. When the main auditorium is finished, it will seat 1,000 people.

Arkady's wife, Alla, is head of the Sunday school, with over 300 children from unchurched families every Sunday. She also teaches Bible in the public schools in Minsk. Recently, she has become director of all Sunday schools for the Pentecostal Union in Minsk.

When Olga came to the United States in June 1995, I considered making Sasha Schneerson the general director of our company in Minsk. Sasha, an intelligent attorney, had attended Christ For The Nations Institute in Dallas. He was not quite ready to be the director so I offered the job to Arkady. Sasha worked very hard for another two years and when the time was right, Arkady left and Sasha became our general director. He is a gentleman and a pleasure to work with, and his education is also very helpful in all our legal battles.

In May 1997, our oldest daughter, Julia, graduated from Baylor University with a degree in finance. The following month, Cathy Carter, who had handled our finances for several years, told me she needed to move to East Texas and help her mom. Cathy's father had just passed away and her mom needed help. I asked Julia if she would be interested in doing this job. She said, "Yes." Cathy agreed to train Julia, and we both felt that this was God's timing. Julia has been very faithful in her job.

Our youngest daughter, Marcy, is a junior at Baylor University studying marketing. We pray for God's will in her life, too, and are hoping that when she graduates, she too will work with us.

In March 1999, we will have been working in Minsk eight-and-a-half years. We have printed Christian literature for dozens of countries in many languages, and have printed over 15,000,000 New Testaments, 3,000,000 Bibles, and over 100,000,000 other pieces of Christian literature.

God has allowed us to work in very unusual circumstances. We are now on our third printing of the personal story of General "Robbie" Risner, a pilot in the Vietnam war, shot down and held prisoner during the conflict. As a POW he "lived" in Hanoi Hilton for over six years. In the book, he gives the account of his faith in God. An interesting note is that the book is being purchased by the U.S. government, and is being shipped to over 200 Air Force bases and the Air Force Academy, to be given to each new pilot.

We have just purchased our second web press; each is capable of printing over a railroad car of paper a day. Currently, we are printing over 1,300,000 books for Josh McDowell for Cuba; 700,000 Russian Study New Testaments for Living Stream Ministries; thousands of New Testaments for the Russian Army through Revival Fires; and have just finished printing Azerbaijan and Georgian New Testaments for the Gideons and the Institute of Bible Translation. We have printed thousands of new version Russian Bibles and New Testaments for International Bible Society and World Bible Translation Center. The Bible League has given us our first order of Russian Bibles for our new web press, and we just shipped Romanian Bibles for the Bible League.

We have printed for over 150 different Christian organizations in our plant in Minsk. God has given us many friends that have helped us gather strength to continue. One special friend is Ralph Bradshaw of International Correspondence Institute. Ralph ran a four-color press for many years before going to work at ICI. Two different years, he donated his vacation time and spent it in Minsk, helping us improve our four-color quality. Without the love and prayers and tireless efforts of many people like this, our plant could not have survived. My greatest thanks goes to our Lord and Savior, Jesus Christ. He has given purpose and direction both in Shirley's life and in mine.

Chapter Twenty-Five

The Making of a President

By Ginger Lindsay

Dennis was born in the city of Ashland, Oregon, on August 29, 1946, as the third child of Gordon and Freda Lindsay. At the time, his dad and mom pastored an Assembly of God church. Though comfortably fulfilled ministering to a thriving congregation, the family was soon uprooted — off to answer the evangelistic call Gordon received from the Lord. Life in a traveling mobile home preceded the settling of the family in Shreveport, Louisiana, where *The Voice of Healing* magazine was birthed by Gordon and his friend, Jack Moore.

Three years later, Gordon moved the ministry headquarters to Dallas, Texas. From his early years through high school, Dennis remembers entertaining himself by making his own fun. While his parents were busy administrating the growing Christian organization that grew naturally from the success of the magazine, Dennis was discovering his creative ability. Along with a friend, he built a 25-room clubhouse, mostly from the wooden paper skids he acquired from his father's print shop. Providing more adventure was the 18-hole golf course he designed and constructed with whatever he could find in his backyard and the fields surrounding his house. The empty tomato and fruit cans he planted in the ground were suitable for making a hole-in-one! He made his own toys with whatever was on hand. There was no Nintendo nor did store-bought toys fill his bedroom. He accepted the challenge to create his own playground.

When he was about 13, Dennis' dad directed his attention toward astronomy through a gift. Who would have thought that a child's toy could change the course of a life? But the fascinating telescope his dad gave him triggered his curiosity and ultimately an insatiable desire to search into the broader world of science. This led him into the arena of truth in which the Lord would use him to illuminate with simplicity and clarity the complete compatibility of science and the Bible. In college, he immersed himself in the field of scientific study, from which he later drew as he taught at Christ For The Nations Institute.

Dennis' inquisitiveness also led him to take apart radios, small appliances and gadgets, although he was not always able to put them back together. He occupied himself by exploring the world of nature around his neighborhood. On one occasion, he was experimenting with fire, and quickly discovered fire is prone to get out of control easily, especially on a windy day. As he was trying to stomp out the spreading fire, his mom looked out the kitchen window. In horror, she immediately took spiritual authority over the fire to stop, then called the fire department. Before the firemen arrived, the fire had spread along the whole side of the house from the backyard to the front yard, but stopped just before burning the wall of the house.

Dennis witnessed so many miracles of God during the 1950s in his father's and other healing evangelists' crusades, that he thought miracles were the normal result of prayer in a Christian's life. Legs grew out, deaf ears were opened, blind eyes saw, people were raised out of wheel chairs, and arm and leg braces came off as limbs were healed.

He was also present when his father's gift of knowledge was not functioning accurately. One day when he got in trouble, his father came into his bedroom to spank him. He scrambled under the bed where his dog, Mimi, happened to be resting in solitude. As his dad began swinging his belt under the bed in an effort to wallop him, Dennis came up with the idea to squeeze Mimi until she yelped. His dad stopped, satisfied that he had successfully carried out his intentions.

After graduating from Adamson High School in Oak Cliff, Dennis attended the University of Texas at Arlington. A life-changing and embarrassing experience he'll never forget occurred in English class as the teacher asked whether anyone still believed in the biblical creation account. Along with another student, Dennis sheepishly raised his hand at half mast. The teacher was incredulous that any of her students would believe such a preposterous fantasy! Dennis realized then that he didn't have a reasonable explanation for believing the biblical account except that the Bible said so. It was then that he determined to discover why he believed God created all things.

The next several years, Dennis divided his time between his college studies, sports, and surfing at the beach near his new alma mater, Southern California College in Costa Mesa, California. He was elected president of his senior class.

During the summer of 1967, before his last year of college, God directed Dennis to participate in a YWAM outreach to the Caribbean, where he preached for the first time in Jamaica. It proved to be another life-changing experience. He returned to SCC and added Bible to his major, graduating with a minor in science.

Had he not gone on the Caribbean outreach, Dennis wouldn't have attended SCC an additional year, nor would he have majored in Bible. It was during his last year at SCC that he met his Swedish-German blonde, college sweetheart, Ginger Krickbaum.

The first week of college included the fanfare of welcome week, aimed at quickly acquainting the underclassmen with the upperclassmen. The SCC Dating Game (patterned after the television Dating Game) matched Dennis and Ginger. By virtue of his office of senior class president, Dennis was one of the three available bachelors participating in the game. As a freshman, Ginger was asked to assume the bachelorette role. Ginger chose Dennis because he didn't try to impress her with his answers as did the other two. His transparency impressed her. They were sent to a live concert at Melodyland across from Disneyland.

Smitten, Dennis and Ginger continued their courtship through the year, until his spring graduation released him to return home to Dallas, where he worked for the summer in preparation to join Youth With a Mission for a year. At that time YWAM, founded by Loren and Darlene Cunningham who were based in Lausanne, Switzerland, was in the pioneering stage.

Ginger completed another year of studies at SCC while Dennis immersed himself in missions, evangelism and personal discipleship classes in the School of Evangelism in Lausanne. After finishing the intense program, his class was presented with many opportunities for practical application of the truths they had learned as they were bused through Europe and the Middle East. They experienced the journeys of Paul the Apostle in Greece, Turkey and Italy and walked in the footsteps of Jesus and His disciples in Israel.

In April 1970, near the end of Dennis' training program in Lausanne, he and Ginger felt the time was right to plan their wedding for the end of the summer, when he would be finished with the year's program. He purchased a set of rings he designed while in Lausanne. His mom advised them to marry on his birthday to help him remember their anniversary.

Dennis returned to California after 14 months away — a week before the wedding. He was quite thin and didn't have a cent to spare.

The girl Dennis married, Ginger Fay Krickbaum, was born on July 8, 1950, the second born of a young Pentecostal couple, Clark and Mildred ("Millie") Krickbaum. They were living in Cheyenne, Wyoming, where the Wind Festival runs January 1-December 31. Cheyenne was also known as train country. Ginger's father and her Christian grandfather were both employed by the Union Pacific Railroad.

On one occasion, Ginger and her brother, Corky, rode in a huge locomotive with their grandfather, who was the engineer from Cheyenne to Scottsbluff, Nebraska. They were spellbound as they watched the single, powerful light in front of the engine illuminate antelope and other wildlife in the snow, swiftly crisscrossing the railroad tracks ahead of them. Corky and Ginger eagerly tugged on the handle that blew the shrill train whistle.

Ginger's parents both worked full time; Clark was a traffic rep and Mildred a bookkeeper. Ginger's father transferred to several other locations: from Cheyenne to Salt Lake City, Utah, to Long Beach, California, and back to Cheyenne, where Ginger spent most of her public school years.

Although generally quiet, Ginger relished her involvement in school with the student government, track, and quarterbacking football. She also enjoyed participating in church events and drama productions — resigning herself to years of piano instruction and piano recitals at the behest of her mother who played the piano, organ and accordion at church.

Ginger has always loved to travel, which probably began with the early school holidays and summers that provided her and her brother with a unique opportunity to ride the Union Pacific passenger trains free any time, anywhere, as long as there were seats available. So when holidays came, Corky and Ginger were often sent to visit various relatives. Those were the days when it was safe for two fairly responsible kids, who were loaded with instructions and ultimatums from Mom and Dad and under the oversight of the train's conductor, to ride for several days across the country from Oregon to California to Nebraska.

The first order of the journey was always to explore the train from stem to stern. What an adventure for two kids to eat in and maintain their balance walking through a swaying, halting dining car without knocking any dinnerware items over (which they mastered), and sleeping with the screeching, rhythmic sounds of the wheels rolling over the tracks. Reading and napping in the quiet second floor observation deck with the adults was their break from activities. Most scary of all was crossing each of the formidable, jerking, outside passageways connecting the train cars, but, oh, what fun!

When Ginger entered high school, she was involved in several arenas of competition in which she was successful. While a sophomore in high school, she was selected from among 12 interviewees as the State DeMolay Sweetheart of Wyoming in Cody, Wyoming.

Upon accompanying her parent's transfer to California (for the second time) in the middle of her junior year of high school, Ginger experienced the limelight again at Fountain Valley High School in the homecoming court.

Unbeknown to the students at Fountain Valley High School, a talent scout from Disneyland was working incognito at the school as a music instructor. He initiated Disneyland's approach to Ginger to become employed as their first Cinderella on parade. After two consecutive summers and a winter of helping to fulfill the dreams of thousands of children living in a fantasy world, Ginger graduated from high school an honor student. She then pursued her desire to study psychology and political science at SCC — now Vanguard University — where she met her "Prince Charming."

Two years after they met, Ginger and Dennis were married in Westminster, California. Gilbert, Dennis' brother, loaned them his Corvette and gas credit card for their traveling honeymoon. Ginger had acquired a small savings while working after her classes, and saved a couple hundred dollars beyond her personal expenses for the honeymoon. They had no idea how much it would cost touring through 15 national parks and forests for three weeks, and decided to stay overnight with a few relatives along the way to stretch their funds.

Four months later, Dennis took his bride to Lausanne, Switzerland to attend the next School of Evangelism with her. Dennis also had oversight of the student work schedule. During the three-month period, Ginger was assigned secretarial duties for Loren Cunningham.

It was difficult adjusting to marriage away from the familiar, living in foreign countries as Americans, eating foreign food, not understanding the foreign languages, and sharing every living area, except the bedroom, with others they didn't know well. Insecurities manifested, doubts and fears overruled for a time, but God came through and what He purposed in their lives was accomplished.

A highlight of their training with YWAM was the three-month tour the leadership mapped out each year for the students at the end of classes. This time both traveled with their 30+ classmates through Italy, the seven churches of Revelation in Turkey, Israel, the islands of Rhodes and Cypress, Bulgaria, Greece and the former Yugoslavia. Each student had written about a biblical site to present upon their arrival to bring the historical significance of the place alive. Ginger researched Mars Hill and Dennis the church at Corinth.

Eating peanut butter sandwiches, sleeping in small pup

tents, living out of suitcases, and washing themselves and their clothes in cold water was not within the comfort zone of the group. But the spiritual and cultural impact and the opportunities to converge on hitchhikers and any other un-suspecting heathen with renewed spiritual savvy, were in themselves rich and invaluable life experiences.

Having experienced a number of challenges in witnessing to all types of people in Europe, Dennis and Ginger had a growing interest in apologetics. They set aside a season to attend L'Abri Fellowship and study under Francis Schaeffer and his team in Huemoz, Switzerland. There they became armed with more tools for witnessing — from the streets to the universities — by learning a reasonable response for their belief. This new grasp on their faith released a new confi-dence that God exists, and that Jesus really is the only way to Him.

The two studied Spanish in Spain until they were able to converse in it. Each summer, for a little under three years, they took a small team of eager evangelistic trainees to Spain from the Swiss YWAM school. After knitting the team together, they thrust them out onto the streets and beaches, into coffeehouses and churches, and into other cities to witness. Spain was a hard country to reach, with its being under the military rule of Generalissimo Franco and the intolerance of Spain's Catholicism, but the Lord faithfully produced fruit for the labor.

In 1972, Dennis and Ginger knew their time in Spain was short and that they would return home soon. Dennis' parents came through Madrid, Spain, just weeks before his dad moved on to heaven. Dennis shared with him their sense that

God's timing for them in Europe was soon coming to a close. When his dad died on April 1, 1973, they immediately returned to Dallas. They discovered Dennis' dad had already paved the way for their return by preparing an open door for him to teach practical Bible classes at CFNI and for Ginger to teach Spanish.

Settled again in Dallas, an unfamiliar nesting instinct catapulted them into parenthood after three years of living out of suitcases in Europe.

Dennis began his career at CFNI as a teacher and the dean of men. He functioned as the dean of families shortly after they began raising their family. While Ginger was pregnant with Missy Joy, she was still teaching Spanish and attending Dallas Baptist University. After another semester of teaching and studying, Ginger retired from teaching and became a full-time mom.

Missy Joy, their oldest child, was described in childhood by Joy Dawson, an internationally gifted speaker, as a "little Dennis with curls." In high school, Missy was deemed the most resourceful of her class, was recognized on the school honor rolls, enlisted as a member of the Trinity Honor Society, and listed in Who's Who of American High Schools.

Missy survived an almost fatal accident in her senior year of high school when a full-size Cadillac ran a red light at a crosswalk just in front of CFNI property, hitting Missy squarely on her side and, upon impact, slamming her face into the windshield of the car. As she flew over the top of the car, the momentum took her about 30 feet on down the street, where she landed. The back of her head opened, and she began bleeding profusely.

Dennis and Ginger had just arrived that same day to minister for a week in a CFN school in Cordoba, Argentina. The evening of the accident, Dennis spoke at a Sunday evening service, and his message was entitled, "God Takes Care of His Children." When they were finally contacted from Dallas, the question before them was, "Will you now trust God with your daughter's life?" Missy was laying on the street thousands of miles away, and when her vital signs were checked, had been pronounced dead. Would they be obedient and stay in Argentina to fulfill God's purposes for the week? They knew God had called them both to be there. Initially Ginger was filled with fear and panic, but after they read Psalms 91 together and prayed over Missy, Dennis turned over in bed and went to sleep. Ginger struggled on into the early morning.

The next morning, Ginger knew the answer was yes; they would trust God to sovereignly care for His daughter! The peace of God overwhelmed her as she realized it was a supernatural intervention in her heart. Calmly they faced the week, knowing God was up to something at home.

Missy's vital signs returned after approximately eight minutes, and an ambulance took her to the hospital. Although she couldn't see or stand on her feet, the MRI and X-rays came out negative — twice — no broken bones, no damage to her organs or her brain. The Lord began healing her, to the amazement of the doctors, and they released her after three days in intensive care. She met Dennis and Ginger at the airport at the end of the week on crutches, with stitches, and bruised from head to foot. The front of her head was still swollen when she went back to school the following week on her crutches, but her vision was pretty much restored. She graduated the following May close to the top of her class. What was God saying to Missy? "I love you, not because of who your parents and grandparents are, but because you're you, and I have a purpose for your life you've yet to fulfill. I am in control."

The accident changed Missy's whole focus on life, filled her with the fear of the Lord, and knit her wayward heart to the Lord's, for she had seen that He does take care of His children.

Missy went on to graduate from Christ For The Nations Institute and later from Oral Roberts University with a B.A. in organizational interpersonal communications. Maintaining a high GPA, Missy was listed on the Deans and Provost's Lists. She presently is working on a master's program in practical theology at ORU and has benefited from four years of a nearly full scholarship. Each summer for the past five years, Missy has devoted a season of time to evangelism in such countries as Canada, Albania, Botswana, Brazil and Argentina. She enjoys ministry.

Dennis and Ginger's second daughter, Hawni Eve, whose name means "gracious life" (in the original spelling of Hanni or Hani), is an extrovert. Two years younger than Missy, she also was honored in high school in Who's Who in American High Schools, became a member of the National Honor Society, and was consistently on the honor roll throughout her secondary education. Hawni is the pianist of the family and is gifted with a beautiful voice that has contributed to ensembles and choirs in high school and college.

Hawni also graduated from CFNI and continued her

education on a full scholarship at Dallas Baptist University, where she received the President's Award for academic excellence. She graduates May 1999 having earned a B.A. in business administration. Hawni would like to continue her education overseas as the Lord leads and provides. However the Lord may lead Hawni, Dennis and Ginger know she will be a great communicator.

Four years after Hawni was born, Ginger was forming plans to go back to college as soon as it was convenient. About that same time, the Lord revealed to Ginger's heart His alternative: birth another child into the family. Ginger tried to argue, knowing all the while she would yield to His plan for their family. Dennis had been uncertain for some time, but open.

Golan Gordon joined their family October 20, 1982, five years after Hawni, and was named after the Golan Heights in Israel and his grandfather Lindsay. He was born in true Lindsay form, weighing in at just under nine pounds and 22 inches long. Like a typical brother, he teased his sisters as he grew and presented a challenge to his teachers. His temperament, quite similar to his father's, has allowed Golan to be the perfect golfing and basketball companion and competitor for his dad.

Golan has a call of God on his life. Whether he chooses to become a teacher or businessman, he has already revealed a tenderness for God in his heart. Last Christmas, his grandmother Lindsay asked six of her grandchildren what their goal is in life. Most gave social, educational or career-oriented answers; but Golan's response was "to go to heaven."

Some of Dennis and Ginger's most memorable times

together with their family are the summers they traveled to various ministry locations. They took Ginger's parents along, and often met grandmother Lindsay at the destination, thus making a family holiday out of it. What a blessing the kid's grandparents, Clark and Mildred Krickbaum, have been to them through the years; they've been ready at a moment's notice to keep the children while they have traveled. The Krickbaums have made it possible for Dennis and Ginger to go out as a team, develop special ministry relationships, and grow together spiritually through all they've experienced on the mission fields of the world.

In 1985, the Board of Directors of CFN promoted Dennis from vice president to president and CEO of Christ For The Nations. To enhance his skills in his new administrative position, Ginger and he attended a leadership school at University of the Nations in Kona, Hawaii for three months. A few years later, his mom, Freda Lindsay, stepped down as chairman of the board of directors, again relinquishing the reins of another strategic function of CFN to him.

The courses he has developed and taught over 26 years on faculty at CFNI, have mostly been in the area of practics. They include Christian Ethical Behavior, The Goodness of God, Friendship Evangelism, Apologetics, and Christian Family Foundations. He currently teaches Personal Discipleship and his favorite, Creation Science.

Out of his pursuit concerning the compatibility of science and Scripture, Dennis has written 12 books explaining how the Bible harmonizes with all fields of science. There are more books to come in the Creation Science series.

As Dennis and Ginger have traveled overseas, they have

been challenged by some of the "interesting" accommodations, but are so grateful to the Lord for compensating them from time to time for what they have given up in comfort and privacy.

Their first summer in Spain was marked by some major adjustments as they lived in and worked out of a church on the southern coast. Their first bedroom on the mission field was the church office of the pastor with whom they were working. A double blowup mattress with zipped together sleeping bags, a small reclusive lizard, suitcases, and the pastor's desk were the contents of the office at night. Sometime in the middle of each night, the air mattress deflated, and early each morning the bedding and suitcases had to be moved out before the pastor came to work.

Just outside of Madrid, their next bedroom was in a large storage room of the church. It was the only feasible place for semi-privacy, so their bed was made using a child's mattress, held and hiked up from the ground three feet on each end by two dressers and whatever else could be found to put in the middle. The circumstances were too humorous for them to think about feeling sorry for themselves.

Although they have lived in other similar circumstances and have chosen to live in campus housing with the students for the past 25 years, the Lord has surprised them with special treats, such as being assigned to live in a new, beautiful, storybook Swiss chalet while studying at L'Abri Fellowship. They have relaxed at five star hotel accommodations with car, meals, and airline tickets provided free of charge for their stay in Hawaii. They have been able to enjoy the privilege of using quite a few lake houses, mountain condos, and a Swiss mini-mansion without the responsibility of ownership.

Being established in a many-faceted Christian organization has afforded them a variety of God-given opportunities to expand their vision and prove God's faithfulness. When they first returned from YWAM, they broke new ground by instituting a CFNI summer outreach program where they took mission teams from CFNI to Mexico. They partnered with veteran missionaries Wayne Myers and Paul Northrup. These short term outreach events proved invaluable to the discipline and cultural and spiritual development of the individual students as they faced many unknowns on the outreaches that kept them totally dependent on the Lord. Those trips are faith growth spurts for the leaders too.

Another privilege at CFN that has been a blessing to Dennis and Ginger is the opportunity they have had to co-host with Dennis' mother a number of Israel tours on which friends and partners of CFN have joined them. Not only are the awesome, historical sites of the Old and New Testaments visited, but the CFNI graduates in Israel briefly join the tour, sharing their vision and their work with the lost sheep of Israel. Dennis' sister and brother-in-law, who have lived in Israel for 30 years, enlarge on what the Lord is doing today in His land. What a thrill it was on their first visit to Israel to dance in the streets of Jerusalem with the Israelis on their Independence Day! The Lord knit their hearts to Israel as they celebrated with the Israelis. They never tire of seeing the apple of His eye.

A feature of the institute branch of the ministry of Christ For The Nations that they truly value is the exposure they have to mighty, anointed men and women of God who come to address the students each week. These are world leaders in the body of Christ who are on the cutting edge of ministry. They challenge the students and staff with up-to-date reports of all the earth-shaking events in the spiritual and natural realms and of the needy and the persecuted church.

Having traveled to over 50 nations, Dennis and Ginger have seen first hand what the Lord is doing among the rest of the body of Christ, and have been able to minister in many of these cultures. One thing they see clearly is that the Church of Jesus Christ is alive and well — no matter what the circumstances or the country.

Part VI:
Wisdom
for World
Changers

Chapter Twenty-Six

Free Indeed and Heaven Bound!

I. Everyone has only two choices — heaven and hell; two eternal destinies to choose from — eternal life and eternal punishment (Matt. 25:46).

II. "For all have sinned and fall short of the glory of God" (Rom. 3:23).

"There is none righteous, no, not one. ... There is none who seeks after God" (Rom. 3:10,11).

"All we like sheep have gone astray ... and the LORD has laid on Him the iniquity of us all" (Isa. 53:6).

III. Adam and Eve were God's first human creation.

A. God gave them a choice: to obey Him and live in His garden or to disobey Him and be banished from the garden.

1. They chose to believe Satan and disobey (Gen. 3:1-24).

B. The curse came on all humans at birth as a result.

1. No parent needs to teach his children to lie;

            sin is born in them.

       2.   No parent needs to teach his child selfishness or stubbornness; these traits arise early without any instruction.

IV. Repentance to God is the necessary step to being born again.

    A. "Unless you repent you will all likewise perish," Jesus said (Lk. 13:3).

    B. Repentance means to turn in the opposite direction. So unless repentance takes place, you are headed in the direction of hell.

V.   God loves you regardless of your past.

    A. "For God so loved the world that He gave His only begotten Son, that whoever believes in Him should not perish but have everlasting life" (Jn. 3:16).

    B. You can come to God only through His Son, Jesus. That's God's provision. "Jesus said ... 'I am the way, the truth, and the life. No one comes to the Father except through Me'" (Jn. 14:6). "I am the door. If anyone enters by Me, he will be saved, and will go in and out and find pasture. The thief does not come except to steal, and to kill, and to destroy. I have come that they may have life, and that they may have *it* more **abundantly**" (Jn. 10:9,10).

VI. Believe that God has heard you after you have prayed the prayer of repentance.

    A. Jesus said, "And whatever things you ask in

prayer, believing, you will receive" (Matt. 21:22).

VII. You are now a changed son (child) of God.

    A.   "Therefore, if anyone *is* in Christ, *he is* a new creation; old things have passed away; behold, all things have become **new**" (II Cor. 5:17). As soon as you accept Christ, your new life begins. As you mature in your faith, old habits will fall away; your choice of intimate friends will now change; your conversation and vocabulary will be different; your lifestyle will please God. All your choices will reflect the new you.

VIII. Verbally confess your new-found relationship with your family, friends, co-workers — everyone you see.

    A.   "If you confess with your mouth the Lord Jesus and believe in your heart that God has raised Him from the dead, you will be saved. For with the heart one believes unto righteousness, and with the mouth confession is made unto salvation" (Rom. 10:9,10).

IX. Become a vital part of a body of believers — a church or a Messianic congregation — who love Jesus.

    A.   "Not forsaking the assembling of ourselves together … and so much the more as you see the Day approaching" (Heb. 10:25).

X. Be filled with the Holy Spirit.

    A.   Jesus commanded the believers to be filled with the Holy Spirit (Acts 1:4).

XI. Become an active witness to the whole world, which is your summons from God for your entire life.

A. "You shall receive power when the Holy Spirit
    has come upon you; and you shall be witnesses
    to Me in Jerusalem, and in all Judea and Samaria,
    and to the end of the earth" (Acts 1:8)

B. "And He said to them, 'Go into all the world
    and preach the gospel to every creature'"
    (Mk. 16:15).

XII. Live a life that is above reproach before all, starting
     at home.

A. "You will know them (believers) by their fruits.
    ... Every good tree bears good fruit, but a bad
    tree bears bad fruit" (Matt. 7:16,17).

XIII. Things to remember as you share Jesus with others:

A. Always carry a Bible with you or have one
    readily available.

B. Share your faith with the same sex, generally.
    Use caution and wisdom in sharing or praying
    with the opposite sex, especially in private.
    Unbelievers can easily misinterpret your
    concern for them as flirting.

C. Share or pray with those approximately your
    age; they will be the most receptive to you.
    However, God can use you to win those of any
    age to Christ!

D. Keep your heart pure and in tune with God —
    ready to take every opportunity to share Jesus.

Chapter Twenty-Seven

How to Minister the Baptism in the Holy Spirit

I'll give you one surefire ministry: Instruct people how to receive the baptism in the Holy Spirit. If you haven't found your ministry yet, then find it now. The Bible recipe I'm going to give you, added with a little faith, will give you an open door around the world. Believe me, it's true.

Everywhere I go, I preach the message of the baptism in the Holy Spirit. This is one that always brings results. Get this message in your heart. People from all over the world who have attended Christ For The Nations Institute and have heard and used this message, get results.

Of course, we turn to the book of Acts to learn about the infilling of the Holy Spirit. We're going to see whether speaking in tongues is a necessary sign of being filled with the Holy Spirit.

What would you say of a person who can't pray in tongues and yet claims he's received? I'd say he is bound. It's just that simple. I notice Kenneth Hagin, Oral Roberts and other leaders are fluent in tongues. Most of the men of God who are really out there doing something for God pray very fluently in tongues. I've stood beside them on the platform or wherever. They are almost continually praying in tongues.

Let's begin with Acts 1:4. It says of the Lord Jesus, "And being assembled together with *them* (the disciples)." Remember, they had been three years with the Lord. You would think He'd have taught them everything they needed to know, but He had something yet to tell them — about the infilling of the Holy Spirit.

Imagine studying in the Lord's Bible school for three years. Then, when He's getting ready to leave to go to heaven, He tells you there is one thing more you need. He tells you about the infilling of the Holy Spirit, and He *commands* you to receive.

Sometimes I hear people say, "Well you know, God knows where I live. If He wants to fill me, let Him go ahead." Yes, He does know where you live. Or, "Well, when God gets good and ready." God has been good and ready for 2,000 years; you are just a little late, though, in following His command. Look at the word *commanded* in your Bible and circle it. He *commanded* them to wait for the Holy Spirit.

Acts 1:8 gives good reasons for being filled with the Holy Spirit: "You shall receive **power** when the Holy Spirit has come upon you; and you shall be **witnesses**." Two good reasons: receiving power and being witnesses.

Do you think Jesus knew He was getting ready to go to heaven? Generally, folk answer, "Yes." If you knew you were going to heaven, what would you say to those you love most? I know what I would say. I would call my children and grandchildren, if they were around, and I would have some-thing to say to Dennis and to Gil and to Carole. I'd have something to say to their families.

I wouldn't say to Dennis, "Now, Hon, be sure after I'm gone to cut the grass." I wouldn't say to Carole (*Shira* in Hebrew, which also means *a song*), "Honey, be sure to keep the silverware polished after I'm gone." No, I would talk about very important things. I would say, "Children, I've done my best to raise you in the fear and admonition of the Lord. I want you to meet me in heaven, but I don't want you to come alone. I want you to bring as many with you as you can." I'd say something like that.

Now this was the Lord's very last message, and what do you think He was talking about? You're right — the infilling of the Holy Spirit (Acts 1:8). So that shows the value, the significance, Jesus placed upon Him. The very next verse says, "Now when He had spoken these things, while they watched, He was taken up, and a cloud received Him out of their sight" (ver. 9). The very last subject Jesus talked about was receiving the infilling of the Holy Spirit.

According to verse 15, we know there were 120 seated together in an upper room, waiting. The Lord told them to wait right there until they received the infilling of the Holy Spirit.

Who all were there? Verse 14 tells us Mary, the mother of Jesus, was there and His flesh and blood brothers as well. (Matthew 13:55 lists his brothers: James, Joses, Simon and Judas.) They were among the 120, and a little later on, we find all 120 received.

We should remember that the natural brothers of Jesus

were not His fans before His resurrection; they were not believers. John 7:3-5 tells us: "His brothers therefore said to Him, 'Depart from here and go into Judea, that Your disciples also may see the works that You are doing. For no one does anything in secret while he himself seeks to be known openly. If You do these things, show Yourself to the world.' For even His brothers did not believe in Him."

As to when they had the revelation that Jesus was indeed their Messiah, we are not told. It might well have been when He rose from the dead. At any rate, we see "His brothers" were among those who were filled with the Holy Spirit on the day of Pentecost (Acts 1:14; 2:4).

When I realized that godly Mary, Jesus' mother, needed to be filled with the Holy Spirit, I said, "If she needed Him, then who am I to resist being filled?"

There are seven instances in the book of Acts which tell us about individuals receiving the Holy Spirit. Let's see now, in fact, how many instances there were in which the individuals receiving spoke in tongues. The Bible says, *"By the mouth of two or three witnesses every word may be established"* (Matt. 18:16).

Acts 2:4 says, "They were **all** filled." So the Lord had enough power to go around, and they were all filled. Put a "1" by verse 4. "They were all filled with the Holy Spirit and began to speak with other tongues." Yes, the Bible records every one present on that day spoke in tongues.

Turn now to Acts 4:31 and put a "2" by it. Here Peter and John had just been released from prison. I like verse 23 which says, "Being let go, they went to their own company" (KJV). A Christian, if he is walking in the light of the Word, will immediately gravitate to people of his kind. If he is spiritual, he will gravitate to the spiritual; if he is carnal, he will automatically seek out carnal companions just like himself.

Peter and John went to other believers and began to tell what God had done. In verses 25 and 26, they were speaking forth the Word from Psalm 2:1,2. When they had prayed, the place was physically shaken. Then those who were assembled together were all filled with the Holy Spirit, and they spoke the Word of God with boldness. In this second instance in which the people were all filled with the Holy Spirit, it doesn't mention they spoke in tongues. So we have one and one. (This does not necessarily mean they did not speak in tongues.)

The third instance is found in Acts 8:18. Put a "3" by that verse, so that anytime you are instructing people how to receive the Holy Spirit, you can quickly turn to this reference.

Now Philip was not a preacher; he was a deacon. He went down to Samaria and began to feel the Spirit of God moving him to tell about the Messiah. Great miracles were taking place. Peter and John, hearing of the miracles occurring under Philip's ministry, came down to assist him. There was great joy in the city.

Simon, a sorcerer, a magician, saw what was happening, and in verse 13 the Bible says, "Simon himself also believed; and when he was baptized he continued with Philip." He has gone this far: he has believed and he has been baptized.

When Peter and John arrived to help Philip, "They ... prayed for them (the believers) that they might receive the Holy Spirit. For as yet He had fallen upon none of them. They had only been baptized in the name of the Lord Jesus. Then laid they hands on them, and they received the Holy Spirit. And when Simon **saw** that through the laying on of the apostles' hands the Holy Spirit was given, he offered them money" (Acts 8:15-18).

Simon *saw* something. What did he see? If nothing had happened, why would he want this gift? He saw some phenomenon that impelled him to make this offer to Peter, John and Philip: "Give me this power also" (ver. 19), and I'll give you some money. He thought it would be neat to add to his bag of tricks the ability to lay hands on people, and they would burst out speaking in tongues. It had to have been that. What other interpretation could one have?

Now Peter spoke to him, "Your money perish with you, because you thought that the gift of God could be purchased with money!" (ver. 20). That phrase *gift of God* is very important. The Holy Spirit is a gift.

Here we see Simon who has believed, has been baptized, and then he saw that when the disciples laid their hands on people something happened. Does the Scripture say the people spoke in tongues? No, so we won't count that. We now have one instance where Scripture says they spoke in tongues; two where it does not mention it.

Turn to Acts 9:17 and put a "4" there by that Scripture. This is the story of Saul, who had been persecuting the Church. On his way to Damascus, Syria, a brilliant light beamed down upon him, he fell to the ground, and Jesus spoke to him. Saul was blind for three days. Ananias was sent by God to Saul to welcome him and to pray for him.

Ananias was anxious; he seemed to think that the Lord had not heard this was the same Saul who was persecuting the Christians. Nonetheless, the Lord told him to go and pray with Saul, who was later called *Paul*. "Ananias went his way and entered the house; and laying his hands on him, he said, 'Brother Saul, the Lord Jesus, who appeared to you on the road as you came, has sent me that you might receive your sight and be filled with the Holy Spirit.' Immediately there fell from his eyes *something* like scales, and he received his sight at once; and he arose and was baptized" (Acts 9:17,18).

Does Acts 9:17 say Paul spoke in tongues? No, but did Paul, in fact, speak in tongues? Yes. In I Corinthians 14:18 Paul said, "I thank my God I speak with tongues more than you all." So we have two and two.

The fifth instance is found in Acts 10:46. Put a "5" there. We find Peter at Joppa. (I have been to Joppa many times. The guides show the traditional rooftop right next to the sea where it is said Peter lived.) Peter came home and was hungry. Verses 9 and 10 says while lunch was being prepared, he went up to the rooftop where he began to pray, and the Lord gave him a vision that showed him that God is no respecter of persons. While he was pondering about the vision the Spirit told him about three men coming to see him (ver. 19). The Lord had just admonished him not to call anything unclean, and almost immediately, three gentiles arrived at his door. Cornelius, an Italian, had sent them to bring Peter back.

I like what Cornelius did. It says that while Cornelius (ver. 24) was waiting for Peter and the three men to return, he called together his relatives and close friends because he didn't want to hear the Good News alone. He wanted to share it with his family and friends. I love people who are unselfish and want to share the Gospel, the Good News!

So Peter preached to this group, and as he spoke (ver. 44), the Holy Spirit fell on them. "Those of the circumcision who believed were astonished, as many as came with Peter, because the gift of the Holy Spirit had been poured out on the Gentiles also. For they heard them speak with tongues and magnify God" (ver. 45,46). So now we have three instances where the Scriptures say they spoke in tongues and two where it does not.

The sixth instance is recorded in Acts 13:52. Here in the town of Iconium, evangelists Paul and Barnabas were preaching. They had been rejected by the Jews in Antioch and after shaking the dust off their feet, they went to Iconium. The Bible simply states the believers were filled with joy and with the Holy Spirit. Does it say they spoke with tongues? No. So in building our case, we have three and three.

Let's see what the last account of folk receiving the Holy Spirit says in Acts 19:6. Put a "7" beside that verse in your Bible. Paul is preaching at Ephesus, and he asked, "'Did you receive the Holy Spirit when you believed?' So they said to him, 'We have not so much as heard whether there is a Holy Spirit'" (Acts 19:2).

"And when Paul had laid hands on them, the Holy Spirit came upon them, and they spoke with tongues and prophesied" (Acts 19:6). All received — every one of the 12 people present. Does it say they spoke with tongues? Yes.

Now we have four instances where the recipients spoke with tongues. They received without tarrying, without waiting, without agonizing and without exception. From the Bible, I believe we have proved our case that speaking in tongues is the initial sign of the infilling of the Holy Spirit. We needed two or three witnesses to prove our case (Matt. 18:16), and we have four. Case won!

Some denominations believe that one receives the Holy Spirit the moment he accepts Christ as Lord. When I begin to instruct on the Holy Spirit, I never let folk ask questions. You can get into all sorts of arguments about doctrinal differences. If someone says, "I want to ask you a question," I answer, "Please, just wait until after you have received, then you may ask your questions." Rarely do they ask any questions afterward. They already have their answer from the Lord. Be in control in a godly way, in the Spirit of Christ, while you are instructing. Let the compassion and love of the Lord guide you. Remember, you are there to help people.

Acts 2:4 says, "They were all filled with the Holy Spirit and began to speak with other tongues, as the Spirit gave them utterance." I ask this question, "*Who* began?" Sometimes people answer, "The Holy Spirit." That is not what this Scripture says. It says *they* (the people) began to speak with other tongues as the Spirit gave them utterance. That is where a lot of folk have a hang-up.

When I gave my heart to the Lord at age 18, I had to believe Jesus forgave my sins and wrote my name in heaven. It took an act of faith.

When I had tuberculosis in both lungs at the age of 24, I had to believe that when Gordon and I prayed together, the Lord heard our prayer. The doctor held my X-rays up to the window in my mother's living room and said, "Young lady, I have bad news for you. You have TB in both lungs." After prayer, I had to believe all was changed and that the Lord had now delivered me. It took an act of faith.

When I received the infilling of the Holy Spirit, it took an act of faith. What is an act of faith? It is like jumping off a diving board. You are never going to get wet until you actually make the leap. The leap in this case is: You begin speaking.

When I speak in English, I use *my* lips, *my* tongue, *my* teeth, *my* voice. When I speak in tongues, I do the same: I use *my* lips, *my* tongue, *my* teeth, *my* voice. I must begin.

My little mother was Lutheran when our family came into the Charismatic renewal. My father received the Holy Spirit instantly, as did most of the grown children. But the devil told Mother she wasn't good enough. Now what she ever did that was so bad she could not be filled with the Holy Spirit, I will never know. Because with 12 children, washing on a washboard, she did not even have time to read the funny papers. But for 35 years, the devil was telling her, "You are not good enough." The devil will try to cheat you out of everything God has for you. Also, she was waiting for the Holy Spirit to "zap" her and make her speak. But the Holy Spirit is a gentleman; He will never make you speak. You must take the step of faith; you must begin.

You have to use your lips, tongue, teeth and voice. That is a most important piece of information you will share with those who want to receive the Holy Spirit. They must take that step of faith.

The only condition for receiving the infilling of the Holy Spirit, and this is important, is that you must be born again. Sometimes, I have seen as many as 250 come to receive the Holy Spirit at one time. I always lead them in a sinner's prayer, because I am sure that out of that large a group, there will be someone without salvation. Any time I have doubt about whether a person seeking the Holy Spirit is saved, I lead him or her in the sinner's prayer. Then I know the individual is ready. When my mother finally realized she had to do the speaking, she opened her mouth and began to speak in tongues. And for the rest of her life until she died at age 87, she prayed in tongues every day.

A lot of friends say, "I received the Holy Spirit when I became a Christian." I tell them, "That is fine; how long have you been a Christian?" "Five years." What would you think if I came to your house, stayed there for five years, and never said a word? That would be very strange. The fact of the matter is, the Holy Spirit is a Person. He will speak for Himself if you give Him an opportunity. But it is a joint venture. You must supply the lips, tongue, teeth and voice, and the Holy Spirit who took up residence within you when you were born again, will begin to give you the utterance. He will give you the words to say. You do not think or plan with your mind what you are going to say. This comes from the Holy Spirit.

When I start to pray with people, I ask them not to say one word in English or their native tongue. If they are expecting to speak in tongues, there is no point in speaking in another language. One cannot speak two languages at once.

I can speak a little German, but I cannot simultaneously speak in English. I have to choose one or the other. I instruct people, "Don't speak in your native tongue because you cannot speak two languages at once. As you open your heart, as you reach out in faith, the Holy Spirit within you will give you the words to say." (The only reason Christians do not receive is because of ignorance, fear or prejudice.)

I would say that the greatest thing next to salvation that ever happened to me was that I was filled with the Holy Spirit. I remember as a child in Canada, I was very, very timid. We had a large house and a big table for 14, counting Mom and Dad. The table was long, and my mom covered it with old-fashioned oilcloth in the place of white linen. When neighbors would visit us, I would always scoot under the table. I was afraid of people. I always wanted to hear what everyone was saying, but I did not want them to talk to me.

Our family had nothing going for it. After we moved from Canada to the United States, we were very poor. The children at school learned my father was a German immigrant from White Russia and that neither my mom nor dad could speak English properly. I developed a fear of people, afraid they would reject me because we were poor, and because Mom and Dad were not Americans as most of the other children's parents were. So I was just timid.

When the Holy Spirit came upon me, my whole nature changed. It was just wonderful. Yes, the most important event that happened in my life after salvation was that the Lord filled me with the Holy Spirit and made me a brand-new person.

He will only make a brand-new person of you if every day you will release yourself to pray in tongues. Every morning before I leave my apartment, I pray in tongues. It is as automatic as breathing when I wake up. The first thing I do is burst out praying in tongues.

Praying in tongues is the perfect way to pray. Praying in

tongues is the way God would have you pray; for you are actually speaking God's will when you pray in tongues.

Praying in tongues helps you pray unselfishly. When I pray in English, I may pray a selfish prayer. My world is small. I pray for my children, my grandchildren, for the students, the graduates, the faculty, the staff, the board, the advisory council, for CFN outreaches in 120 nations. I pray for the 40 Bible schools we have helped to start. But my world is still small in comparison with the Lord's. When I pray in tongues, I am available to the Lord to pray for anyone, any child of God who needs my prayers that day, for any group or any situation. Yes, praying in tongues is the perfect way to pray.

A most important point, is always to remember to instruct people that the Holy Spirit is a *gift*. Study these Scriptures: Acts 2:38,39; 8:20; 10:45; 11:17. They speak of the Holy Spirit as a gift. You cannot earn a gift. Suppose I offered a $100 bill to you as a gift. How long would it take you to reach for that gift? Not very long. That is how long it should take an individual to receive the gift of the Holy Spirit. You do not need to beg, cry or plead.

Through Christ For The Nations' supporters, we once helped a small Charismatic congregation in Yugoslavia with the finances to restore a beautiful old Jewish synagogue to use for their church. A couple of years later, an invitation from Yugoslavia encouraged me to visit several churches there.

As we were driving down a long street in Osijek, suddenly a beautiful synagogue appeared at the end of the street. Immediately, to my joy and surprise, I recognized it as the synagogue CFN had helped restore. A conference was scheduled there, and I was to speak a couple of times.

On Saturday night, I spoke on the infilling of the Holy Spirit, and the altar was crowded with candidates. Since I didn't understand the Yugoslavian language, I couldn't tell who had received and who hadn't. But several ministers who were praying among the candidates assured me virtually everyone was speaking in tongues.

The next morning, Sunday, it was my turn to speak again. No sooner had I started, when a man, about half-way back in the audience, stood to his feet and began to sob and laugh uncontrollably. The pastor interpreted for me: "Never since I lost both of my arms in the last war have I had one moment of joy or peace. Last night, I came forward and was filled with the Holy Spirit. I went home and went to bed, but couldn't sleep. All night I laughed and cried with joy!"

It was then I noticed his "arms" which he was raising to glorify God were merely crude hooks!

The Bible says in Acts 13:52: "And the disciples were filled with joy and with the Holy Spirit."

I remember one time I was speaking at our Christian Center on the baptism in the Holy Spirit, and I held up a $5 bill at the close of my instruction. I said, "The Holy Spirit is a gift. Here is a $5 gift, and it is genuine. Anyone who wants it, can have it." Some students snickered and some laughed.

A great big Scotsman in the back of the room watched me closely as I held up the $5 bill and kept waving it. Suddenly, I saw him running toward the front. But just then another fellow about the third row from the front decided he wanted it. He moved out of his seat and sort of lumbered toward me.

The big fellow from the back passed up this student and grabbed the $5 bill out of my hand. All the students roared! The loser returned to his seat, slapped his forehead and moaned, "I needed that $5 so badly." I chided, "Look, you were right here up front. Why didn't you come and get it? You were not nearly as far back as the fellow on the last row."

Do you know how he answered? He said, "I just didn't think you meant it."

Many people, including some ignorant or prejudiced preachers, read the Bible, and they do not believe the Lord means what He said. He does mean it, and the Holy Spirit is for you today.

Chapter Twenty-Eight

How to Receive Your Healing

G ordon used to say, "One miracle is worth a thousand sermons."

God's plan for man: "Let them have dominion" (Gen. 1:26).

Satan's plan for man: "To steal, and to kill, and to destroy" (Jn. 10:10).

The curse: "If you do not obey the voice of the LORD your God ... curses will come upon you" (Deut. 28:15).

The cure: "For as many as are of the works of the law are under the curse; for it is written, *'Cursed is everyone who does not continue in all things which are written in the book of the law, to do them.'* ... Christ has redeemed us from the curse of the law, having become a curse for us" (Gal. 3:10,13).

Sickness can come for many reasons — worry, stress, pressure, complaining, unforgiveness, bitterness, unbelief, fear, improper care of your body (not enough sleep, lack of exercise and an unhealthy diet), sin, overwork, drugs, alcohol, smoking and so forth. Sometimes generational curses need to be broken.

How does God heal?

1. His Word. "He sent His word and healed them" (Psa. 107:20). Sometimes God speaks healing through one of His servants (Matt. 8:8). And sometimes His Word — the Bible — is the vehicle of healing. When I was dying of TB in both lungs at age 24, God quickened my spirit with these words: "I shall not die, but live, and declare the works of the LORD" (Psa. 118:17).

2. His stripes. "By His stripes we are healed" (Isa. 53:5). "By whose stripes you were healed" (I Pet. 2:24).

3. Binding and loosing. "Whatever you bind on earth will be bound in heaven, and whatever you loose on earth will be loosed in heaven" (Matt. 18:18).

4. Anointing with oil. "Is any among you sick? Let him call for the elders of the church, and let them pray over him, anointing him with oil in the name of the Lord. ... And the Lord will raise him up" (Jas. 5:14,15).

5. Confession. Confess it with your mouth. "Whatever things you ask when you pray, believe that you receive *them*, and you will have *them*" (Mk. 11:24). "Confess *your* trespasses to one another, and pray for one another that you may be healed" (Jas. 5:16).

6. Believe you receive. "Believe that you receive" (Mk. 11:24 — my husband's favorite verse).

7. Laying on hands. "They will lay hands on the sick and they will recover" (Mk. 16:18).

8. Gifts of healing. "To another gifts of healing" (I Cor. 12:9). In every generation, God has given gifts of healing. Of the several million children of Israel crossing the

desert, the Bible says, *"There was* none feeble among His tribes"* (Psa. 105:37). In the Early Church, there were Peter and Paul and others. In the recent past, there were Smith Wigglesworth and Kathryn Kuhlman. Today, there are several ministers whom God is using in the gifts of healing as Benny Hinn, Reinhard Bonnke, T.L. Osborn and others.

9. Fasting. "*Is* this not the fast that I have chosen? ... Your healing shall spring forth speedily" (Isa. 58:6,8).

10. Covenant of healing. "If you diligently heed the voice of the LORD your God and do what is right in His sight, give ear to His commandments and keep all His statutes, I will put none of the diseases on you which I have brought on the Egyptians. For I *am* the Lord who heals you" (Ex. 15:26).

11. Faith. Those who are "of faith" are Abraham's seed (Gal. 3:7), but Christ is the Mediator of a better covenant, with better promises (Heb. 8:6-8). Since healing was promised under the old covenant, and we now have a new and better covenant, we are surely then entitled to healing.

12. Two or three agreeing. "If two of you agree on earth concerning anything that they ask, it will be done for them of My Father in heaven" (Matt. 18:19).

13. The children's bread. Divine healing is the bread for His children. The Syro-Phoenician woman who had a demon-possessed daughter, pled her case before Jesus by comparing healing to the children's bread. Jesus agreed and healed the child (Mk. 7:26-30). What father would withhold bread from his children?

14. To destroy Satan's works. Jesus healed "all who were oppressed by the devil" (Acts 10:38). He came to "destroy the works of the devil" (I Jn. 3:8).

15. To win souls. Healing is a powerful means of winning souls to Christ. The widow's son died and her faith wavered. But when Elijah raised him from the dead, her faith was restored (I Ki. 17:20,24). Through the apostles of the Early Church, God performed many signs and wonders. Acts 5:14 says, "And believers were increasingly added to the Lord, multitudes of both men and women." Today, most ministers with miracle and healing ministries are seeing multitudes saved.

16. Praise. There's a difference between healings and miracles. Everyone can have faith for healing over a period of time, whereas a miraculous healing takes place immediately. When people would come to Gordon and say, "I've tried everything," he would then ask, "Have you tried the praise cure? It's a sure cure."

17. His will. Christ heals because it is His will. When the leper came to Jesus for healing, he was the only one who ever questioned God's will for healing. The Lord settled the matter once and for all by answering, "I will," and healed him (Matt. 8:3). Gordon used to ask, "If people don't believe it's the Lord's will to heal them, then why do they go to physicians? To get out of God's will?" Erratic logic!

18. One with Christ. Believers are part of Christ's body (I Cor. 12:27). Do you believe that Christ went around with a sick body?

19. Bride without blemish. Christ is coming back for His bride (Rev. 21:9). Will that bride be sickly and diseased? No! No! Gordon used to say, "You don't have to be sick to die."

20. Stand on His Word. Gordon and I stood on the Bible promises for ourselves and our children. Now I'm standing for our eight grandchildren. None of us has ever needed to spend even one day in the hospital — except we mothers when we gave birth to our children, and Missy, my granddaughter who was struck by a speeding car, pronounced dead and was rushed to the hospital. God raised her from the dead. This May she graduates from Oral Roberts University.

21. To glorify God (Jn. 11:4).

Like Gordon used to say, "I'm not laying up for a rainy day, because I'm not going to have any." And he didn't! God took him in an instant.

Chapter Twenty-Nine

God's Financial Plan

Beloved, I pray that you may prosper in all things and be in health, just as your soul prospers (III Jn. 2).

A braham was the first recorded in the Bible to pay tithes. His nephew, Lot, and other Jewish families had been taken hostage by four heathen kings. Abraham rescued them and in gratitude to God, gave the priest, Melchizedek, a tithe (one-tenth) of all he recovered (Gen. 14:14-20).

Isaac planned to go to Egypt because there was a famine in the land of Israel. But God specifically commanded him to stay in Israel, and He would bless him. Did it work? The Bible confirms that in obedience, "Isaac sowed in that land, and reaped in the same year a hundredfold; and the LORD blessed him. The man began to prosper, and continued prospering until he became very prosperous. ... So the Philistines envied him" (Gen. 26:12-14).

Jacob, Abraham's grandson, gives us the second Bible record of tithes paid. After deceiving his father, Isaac, to get the birthright blessing, Jacob fled from his brother, Esau, who now hated him. His first night away from home, through a dream, the deceiver's life was changed. He made a covenant with the Lord: "If God will be with me, and keep me in this way that I am going, and give me bread to eat and clothing to put on, so that I come back to my father's house in peace, then the LORD shall be my God. ... And of all that You give me I will surely give a tenth to You" (Gen. 28:20-22). God kept Jacob and greatly prospered him.

God, being all wise, gave specific plans to mankind how to sustain, insure and provide the means essential for the continued advancement of the truth. In the second book of the Bible, Exodus, God commands, "The first of the firstfruits of your land you shall bring into the house of the LORD your God" (Ex. 23:19). And on and on in the next two books, Leviticus and Numbers, God gives explicit commands regarding tithes and offerings. In fact, so specific is God that He continues: "If a man wants at all to redeem (borrow) *any* of his tithes, he shall add one-fifth to it" (Lev. 27:31). Pretty high interest! Right? Cheaper to borrow from a bank!

Then in the fifth book of the Bible, Deuteronomy, God gives some really thrilling promises of prosperity if we carefully keep His Word: "The Lord will open to you His good treasure. ... You shall lend to many nations, but you shall not borrow. And the LORD will make you the head and not the tail" (28:12,13). Read Deuteronomy 28:1-14. It's exciting!

King David was also an example of giving. He said, "For the house of my God I have prepared with all my might ... my own special treasure of gold and silver. ... Then the leaders of the fathers' *houses*, leaders of the tribes ... captains

... officers ... offered willingly. They gave for the work of the house of God. ... And whoever had *precious* stones gave *them* to the treasury of the house of the LORD. ... Then the people rejoiced, for they had offered willingly ... to the LORD; and King David also rejoiced greatly" (I Chr. 29:2,3,6-9). What a marvelous example of giving in preparing for the building of the temple!

Nehemiah 12:43 tells us of the great rejoicing that took place even among "the women and the children" when offerings were given to God as the Jerusalem walls were dedicated.

In Malachi, the last book of the Old Testament, God reminds us again of the importance of paying tithes and giving offerings. He asks: "Will a man rob God? Yet you have robbed Me! But you say, 'In what way have we robbed You?' In tithes and offerings. You are cursed with a curse. ... Bring all the tithes into the storehouse, that there may be food in My house" (Mal. 3:8-10). One "pays" tithes (that's God's tax to provide for His work), the same as a government assesses taxes (now in the U.S., it's 45 percent of one's income) to maintain the nation. Offerings are "given" only after one has paid his tithes.

What has God promised if we obey this command? God vows: "I will rebuke the devourer for your sakes, so that he will not destroy the fruit of your ground, nor shall the vine fail to bear fruit for you in the land" (ver. 11). Think about this: Always God tells us to resist the devil, but now He promises that if we pay our tithes and give our offerings, He, Himself, will rebuke the devourer! That's awesome! Can't lose!

Next we turn to the New Testament. What does God say about tithing here? Again, in the very first book of the New Testament, Jesus, speaking of tithing says, "You pay tithe of mint, anise and cummin, and have neglected the weightier *matters* of the law: justice and mercy and faith. **These you ought to have done**, without leaving the others undone" (Matt. 23:23). Why didn't Jesus say more about tithing? He was speaking to Jews who already knew all the commands about tithing.

Then the writer of Hebrews goes on to say, "Here mortal men receive (present tense) tithes, but there *he receives* them, of whom it is witnessed that he lives" (Heb. 7:8). Paul added, "He who sows sparingly will also reap sparingly, and he who sows bountifully will also reap bountifully. ... God loves a cheerful giver" (II Cor. 9:6,7).

And how about pledges? Is it scriptural to ask people to pledge? Paul thought it was, for he says: "Therefore I thought it necessary to exhort the brethren to go to you ahead of time, and prepare your generous gift beforehand, which *you had* previously promised, that it may be ready as *a matter of* generosity and not as a grudging obligation" (ver. 5). So Paul even sent several brethren to collect the pledges! The individual who wants God's blessing of prosperity, now knows how to receive it.

> Where your treasure is, there your heart will be also (Matt 6:21).

As a personal testimony, I started tithing immediately upon my conversion at age 18. On my first full-time job as a cashier in a large department store, I earned $1.40 a day. I tithed methodically. When Gordon and I were married, we regularly paid our tithes and gave offerings. A year before Gordon went to heaven in 1973, we gave to Christ For The Nations the only free-of-debt home we ever owned. It was sold to help pay for dormitories for our new Bible school here in Dallas. As I have told my three children, "Not one thing have I ever lacked or needed, that God has withheld." Now at age 85, I joyfully declare, "He has kept His Word!" So far as I know, all of my three children and eight grandchildren tithe.

How important is the matter of money? In the Bible there are 2,085 Scripture references on money and only 205 on salvation — 10 times more on money. Not that salvation is less important than finances, but the fact is that how one handles his money usually indicates how he will spend eternity.

> And you shall remember the LORD your God, for *it is* He who gives you power to get wealth (Deut. 8:18).

Chapter Thirty

Guidelines for a Happy Marriage

1. Marry only a believer. The Bible says, "Do not be unequally yoked together with unbelievers" (II Cor. 6:14).

2. Check the background of the groom or bride. Homosexuality is breaking up marriages even among believers, as is addiction to pornography.

3. Insist on a medical examination since AIDS, hepatitis and multiple social diseases are so rampant.

4. Don't hurry to the altar. Get to really know each other first.

5. Always remember that appearance and good manners are important.

6. Manage your money or it will manage you. Financial problems are the number one cause for divorce. Avoid credit cards as a daily crutch, for it often leads to compulsive buying, especially among women. If you can't pay cash, you don't need it — an exception being the purchase of a home or car. Remember: A borrower

is slave to the lender. Budget. Tithe in obedience to God's Word from the day you marry. If you do, God promises blessing; if not, curses (Mal. 3:10-12).

7. Establish bylaws with in-laws. Your first commitment is to your mate. Never make a negative remark about relatives.

8. Discover godly friends you'll both enjoy.

9. When misunderstandings come, don't harden your heart. Talk it over. Don't use the "silent treatment." "Do not let the sun go down on your wrath" (Eph. 4:26).

10. Give each other at least one sincere compliment every day.

11. Never belittle the other person before another.

12. Respect one another.

13. Trust each other. Don't ever lie. You can't keep it secret.

14. Don't take each other for granted. Make a decision to grow closer as the years go by. The better you treat your husband or wife, the more people will respect you.

15. Pray together daily, which multiplies your effectiveness greatly. The Bible says that one shall "chase a thousand, and two put ten thousand to flight" (Deut. 32:30).

16. Never stop courting. Your spouse comes first — ahead of family, business, etc.

17. Maintain good health by forming right habits regarding eating, exercise, sleeping, playing.

18. Build your faith by diligently reading God's Word daily. Satan often attacks believers and their families to reduce their effectiveness for God.

19. Regularly attend God's house — the church.

20. Sex is God-ordained. He planned it for pleasure and purpose. What purpose? God tells us: "Yet she is your companion. ... But did He not make *them* one, having a remnant of the Spirit? And why one? He seeks godly offspring. Therefore, take heed to your spirit" (Mal. 2:14,15). Yes, God our Creator planned it so that a husband and wife in a real sense can help Him create another human being with a divine purpose! Enjoy sex, guard it carefully, and keep it alive.

21. Marriage is a covenant for life between three — man, woman and God. Don't let your love life grow stale. Make it work with God's help and for His glory!

Chapter Thirty-One

Raising Godly Children

G ordon used to say, "If it doesn't work at home, don't try to export it."

- "Behold, children *are* a heritage from the LORD" (Psa. 127:3) — on loan.

- The Lord "seeks godly offspring" (Mal. 2:15).

- Pray for your child while he/she is still in the womb.

- Audibly speak words of blessing to your children in the womb. "Death and life *are* in the power of the tongue" (Prov. 18:21). A newborn recognizes and is often soothed by the sound of a mother or father's voice more quickly than a stranger's voice. Continue to speak blessing over your children throughout their lives.

- Teach your children godly principles from their birth. We're told that children have already formed many of their values for life by age 3. "You shall teach them (God's commandments) diligently to your children, and shall talk of them when you sit in your house, when you walk by the way, when you lie down, and when you rise up" (Deut. 6:7).

- Discipline your children. "He who spares his rod hates his son, but he who loves him disciplines him promptly" (Prov. 13:24). "Foolishness *is* bound up in the heart of a child; the rod of correction will drive it far from him" (Prov. 22:15). (See also 23:13,14; 29:17.)
- Establish family altar with your children from birth, reading God's Word to them and praying with them.
- Teach your children to pray, letting them take turns. Lead them in the sinner's prayer. Instruct them on how to receive the Holy Spirit baptism (Acts 2:39).
- Ask your children to read from God's Word from sections they can understand — as soon as they are old enough to read (II Tim. 3:15). Supply good Christian books for them to read.
- Take your children to church regularly. "Not forsaking the assembling of ourselves together" (Heb. 10:25).
- Help your children memorize special Scriptures (Heb. 8:10).
- Build gratefulness into your children. Teach them to give God thanks (Col. 1:12; 2:7) throughout the day for answered prayers and for daily blessings — even the smallest things. To show them how, point out each time you receive something from God and thank Him aloud before your children.
- Open your home to your children's friends so you can observe them and guide in bringing them to the Lord, or protect your children from them if they are rascals or rebels.
- Get to know the parents of your children's friends. If

your children go to their homes, will there be any
guidelines? Or will they be able to watch anything they
want on TV or the internet, listen to any kind of music,
hear profanity, see drinking, smoking, and possibly
even drug use and pornography?

- Spend quality time with the family, and at times, with
  each child separately. "Through faith and patience
  (we) inherit the promises" (Heb. 6:12).

- Invite your children to talk freely with you — to share
  their joys and their problems. To set the example, talk
  freely with them about matters that concern all of you.

- Keep your children always looking ahead for some
  special occasion: a picnic, birthday party, trip, a game,
  vacation, dinner with friends, a prize for a specific
  accomplishment (Prov. 13:12), a time to play with
  them — games, tennis, ball, golf, swimming.

- When you ask the children to do something, expect
  obedience. Don't tell them, "I'll count to 10 and if you
  don't obey by the time I count to 10, then. ..." This
  will become a joke! Before long, the child will never
  move until you reach 10, and then even begin testing
  you beyond 10.

- Be consistent. Don't disallow something one time and
  allow it the next.

- Teach your children to respect other people, especially
  those in authority — teachers, police, adults, the
  elderly, the sickly, the poor (Deut. 15:7-11), the
  handicapped. They should also be taught respect for
  their parents (Deut. 5:16).

- Don't compare your children with their brothers, sisters, friends, yourself, etc. (II Cor. 10:12).

- Insist on honesty (Prov. 24:26; 12:22). Show your children what God says about liars: "All liars shall have their part in the lake which burns with fire and brimstone" (Rev. 21:8). Remind them of Jesus' Second Coming, and that we will be held accountable to God for our words and our actions.

- Give at least one compliment every day to every member of the family, and teach your children to do the same.

- Teach your children to tithe and give offerings to the Lord's work (Mal. 3:8-10; Matt. 6:19-21; Lk. 6:38).

- Instruct your children on how to handle their allowance — to save a percentage (Prov. 3:9,10; 22:9).

- Tell your children each day that you love them, and show it by your words, actions and embraces.

- Tell your children to choose God's way, the right way in every situation; that their choices will have consequences (Prov. 20:11).

- Remind your children what God says to believe about their children: "All your children *shall be* taught by the LORD, and great *shall be* the peace of your children" (Isa. 54:13).

- Teach your children to respect other people's property and belongings, as well as their own.

- Instill in your children mercy (Col. 3:12), compassion (Lk. 10:30-37), and understanding for others so they will be in line to receive the same.

- Never speak negatively about your children before others, especially if they can hear your negative comments (i.e., "He never obeys me! He's so stubborn").
- Live your life before your children as a good example of integrity (Prov. 11:3) and godliness (Col. 3:1-17).

Chapter Thirty-Two

The Full Man

G ordon used to say, "How a person spends his leisure
time will usually determine his success or lack of it in
life." In his own lifetime, Gordon read thousands of books.
He authored 250 books on many Bible-related subjects.

"Reading maketh a full man, conference a ready man, and
writing an exact man. Knowledge is power," said Francis
Bacon (1561-1626).

Every person has some leisure time. During that special
period, physical exercise should be included. Relaxation
with music or reading can be a special plus.

How often parents fail to realize the importance of reading
for their children. They accommodate their children in many
ways, taking them to games, or watching TV by the hour. Yet
outside of encouraging their offspring to do their homework,
no attempt is made to recommend selected books that would
mature them. Proper choice of reading matter cannot be
overemphasized. Carelessness in this regard can result in the
perversion of a young mind and send him or her on a
downward spiral to hell.

Adults should read too. It's surprising how many Americans are so ill-informed of what goes on even in their own

nation, let alone in the rest of the world. It takes an acquired, disciplined effort to read and keep abreast of events. The *Denver Post* for years carried the slogan, "The world belongs to the one who reads." And I heard one grandfather tell his grandson, "The man who doesn't read will probably dig ditches the rest of his life."

In the earlier years when we first began the ministry of Christ For The Nations, we had an annual summer convention on our property in Dallas. On a display table, we offered Gordon's books. With only a few employees then, and being that it was summer time, I didn't have anyone to run the book table. As I was thinking out loud, Alliene, wife of Wylie Vale, one of our board members and a leading Houston architect (who has designed several of our large buildings), spoke up. "Why not let Shannon run it?"

A little surprised, I questioned, "How old is he? And how would he be able to answer inquiries from the buyers about the books' contents?"

"He's 12, and he's read every book Gordon wrote! He can tell you everything in there," Alliene answered.

So Shannon got the job and did excellent with the sales. (The attraction of a youngster being so well-informed no doubt helped!)

Years have passed. His parents are retired, but I wondered what happened to Shannon and his brother, Wylie Jr., so I phoned their parents. Here's their report:

Shannon was elected to be a partner of the prestigious law firm of Arnold, White & Durkee, which specializes in intellectual properties such as copyrights. He is an exception in the firm: He is the only member who does not have a technical degree. Despite this, he has risen to be one of the top two public relations spokesmen for the firm. He also teaches an adult class in a large Presbyterian church.

Shannon's brother, Wylie Jr. was honored by St. John's prep school with the only award given to a graduate who is not a part of their high school staff or faculty — outstanding graduate of their 50-year existence. Among his achievements: chairman of the professors and a member of the board of trustees at the Salk Institute; the presidency of the International Society of Endocrinology; and the youngest inductee into The National Academy of Science.

Wylie is co-founder, director and chief scientist of the neurocrine biosciences firm that is developing medicines based upon his discoveries in the field of "the brain" research — the latest of which is urocortin, a powerful appetite-suppressing molecule in the hormone family, called Corticotropin Releasing Factor, or CRF.

Such is the story of two brothers whose parents took time to secure books — many informative, some pleasurable — including the Bible and spiritual books by godly authors. The investment has paid rich dividends.

Chapter Thirty-Three

How Not to Build a Church

1. Never start on time; wait till most of the people get there.

2. Leave the front 10 or 15 rows empty.

3. Let the people sit in the back, especially the young people, so they can talk or write notes if they get bored.

4. Don't have a "regular" choir. When the service starts, just invite anybody who wants to sing, to come to the platform and join the choir.

5. Never use any guidelines for choosing those who lead praise and worship; announce that whoever can play an instrument and/or sing is welcome to do so.

6. Let the pastor choose all his or her relatives to run the church and fill the most important positions with them — even if others are better qualified or are gifted in special areas such as — pianist, Sunday school superintendent, youth or worship leader, soloist, etc.

7. The pastor must be "led by the Spirit" — so he should never "prepare" his sermons in advance.

8. If the service runs a bit past the announced time, expect certain members to leave "on time" — so the visitors or the young people will feel free to leave too.

9. After the close of the service, let the children play (bang) on the piano and with the microphones and other sound equipment.

10. Allow each of the children to run to the restroom several times during the service, even if they are seated in the middle near the front of the sanctuary.

11. Kids should feel "at home" in the house of the Lord, so if they want to run back and forth down the aisles or on the altar, give them that freedom.

12. Parents should always bring plenty of cookies, crackers, etc. for the children to eat during services.

13. Gum and candy wrappers and Sunday school papers can be thrown on the floor because the janitor will clean it up.

14. At the close of the service, the pastor must always take his valuable time to speak to that person or persons who monopolize(s) his time, even if that means he won't have time to greet the visitors and others who may really need to speak to him.

15. Don't worry how the church looks inside or out — whether it's clean, the grass is cut, etc., for God doesn't really care; He looks on the "inward" and not on "outward appearances."

16. Don't expect the people to bring their Bibles to church. A lot of the members wouldn't be able to find the sermon Scriptures anyway, because they never read their Bibles,

and they might be embarrassed.

17. Don't urge the members to bring their tithes and offerings to the house of the Lord, for it may offend them. Besides, if they did begin giving, God could start prospering them, which He promised in Malachi 3:8-12. Others seeing this happen might just become interested, start attending the church, get converted, and cause the congregation to grow! Then more workers would be needed to handle the increase.

18. Don't forbid the congregation from bringing soft drinks or coffee and sipping them from time to time throughout the service. You wouldn't want them to be inconvenienced or they might never return.

19. Let the young people sit low in their seats so they can drape their legs over the seats in front of them. This will allow them "freedom" in the house of the Lord.

20. Don't have prayer for the sick. It will make you look bad if the people prayed for aren't healed.

21. Discourage prophecies and words from the Lord by members of your congregation. You are the pastor and all instruction or direction should come from you. Besides, they may be in error, and you might get embarrassed.

22. Don't plan with your ushers the way offerings are to be taken or communion is to be passed around. Just be "led by the Spirit." Call up people at random to be ushers for these times.

23. From the pulpit, read all the announcements that are in your bulletin because some of the members may forget

to read them through the week and would miss out on important events taking place.

24. Parents of infants and toddlers should always sit toward the front. Mothers or fathers with crying infants in their arms should remain seated and rock them to quiet them.

25. Never visit the members of your congregation in their homes. It might make them uncomfortable, and they might have to miss important TV programs, etc.

26 Don't show appreciation for outstanding service of your church members by acknowledging them before the congregation. This might cause jealousy in others.

Chapter Thirty-Four

Why Should I Read the Bible?

by Mike and Hildy Chandler

Although we know that we *should* read the Bible on a regular basis, we sometimes neglect to. Here are some of the reasons why you and I *need* to read God's Word.

- Knowing God's Word helps you know and understand Him.

    You search the Scriptures, for in them you think you have eternal life; and these are they which testify of Me (Jn. 5:39). (See also Jn. 1:1,14; 6:68,69; I Jn. 1:1; 5:20; Rev. 19:13.)

- Reading the Bible will remind you that God is bigger than your circumstances (Ex. 14).

- Regular Bible reading will remind you of God's holiness and help you walk in righteousness.

    Your word I have hidden in my heart, that I might not sin against You (Psa. 119:11).

    How can a young man keep his way pure? By

living according to your word (Psa. 119:9 NIV). (See also II Tim. 3:16,17; Deut. 17:19,20.)

- Knowing God's Word will help you overcome the enemy in times of temptation.

    I have written to you, fathers, because you have known Him *who is* from the beginning. I have written to you, young men, because you are strong, and the word of God abides in you, and you have overcome the wicked one (I Jn. 2:14). (See also Matt. 4:1-11; Eph. 6:17; Gen. 2:16,17; 3:1-4.)

- The Word of God is vital to your existence.

    So He humbled you, allowed you to hunger, and fed you with manna which you did not know nor did your fathers know, that He might make you know that man shall not live by bread alone; but man lives by every *word* that proceeds from the mouth of the LORD (Deut. 8:3). (See also Matt. 4:4.)

- God's Word brings life.

    But Simon Peter answered Him, "Lord, to whom shall we go? You have the words of eternal life" (Jn. 6:68). (See also Jn. 6:63; 8:51; 20:30,31)

- The pure "milk of the word" will help you grow spiritually.

    As newborn babes, desire the pure milk of the word, that you may grow thereby (I Pet. 2:2). (See also I Tim. 4:6; II Tim. 3:16,17; Rom. 10:17.)

- God's Word brings healing and deliverance.

    He sent His word and healed them, and delivered

them from their destructions (Psa. 107:20). (See also Psa. 119:50; Matt. 8:8; Jn. 4:50; 8:31,32.)

- God's Word cleanses us.

  You are already clean because of the word which I have spoken to you (Jn. 15:3). (See also Eph. 5:26; Psa. 12:6,7.)

- Reading the truth will help you walk in the truth.

  The entirety of Your word *is* truth, and every one of Your righteous judgments *endures* forever (Psa. 119:160). (See also Jn. 17:17.)

- God's Word will give you direction, wisdom and strength for your life.

  The entrance of Your words gives light; it gives understanding to the simple (Psa. 119:130). (See also Psa. 119:105; 119:28.)

- Knowing God's Word will help you discern false teaching.

  These were more fair-minded than those in Thessalonica, in that they received the word with all readiness, and searched the Scriptures daily *to find out* whether these things were so (Acts 17:11). (See also Tit. 1:9; II Pet. 1:20, 2:1; II Tim. 2:15.)

- Knowing the Scriptures will give you hope and encouragement, and equip you to be an encourager as well.

  For whatever things were written before were written for our learning, that we through the patience and comfort of the Scriptures might have hope (Rom. 15:4). (See also I Thes. 4:16-18; Acts

20:32.)

- God's Word will bring you joy.

  Your words were found, and I ate them, and Your
  word was to me the joy and rejoicing of my heart;
  for I am called by Your name, O LORD God of
  hosts (Jer. 15:16). (See also Jn. 15:11.)

- The Word of God can "richly dwell in you" through
  regular Bible reading. When it does, you can build up
  others.

  Let the word of Christ dwell in you richly in all
  wisdom, teaching and admonishing one another in
  psalms and hymns and spiritual songs, singing
  with grace in your hearts to the Lord (Col. 3:16).

Chapter Thirty-Five

Qualities of a Godly Leader

G ordon used to say, "A physical or mental breakdown is never in God's plan for a believer."

A godly and wise leader:

1. Must have a plan, a purpose, a goal (Prov. 4:25-27).

2. Takes the initiative — steps forward (Matt. 25:14-30).

3. Recognizes potential in others. Promotes from within organization or church, if possible, searching and praying for qualified persons.

4. Maintains emotional control (Prov. 29:11). Keeps cool even in times of stress.

5. Respects others (I Pet. 2:17). Praises in public; criticizes in private.

6. Is careful in appearance as God's representative (Eccl. 9:8).

7. Controls mouth (Jas. 3:5-12). Weighs his/her words. Makes friends easily.

8. Keeps personal problems to himself/herself.

9. Is able to handle criticism (Prov. 29:1). However, you don't have to answer every critic.

10. Is consistent in example. Daniel had a good record in the hour of his great trial. His accusers, "could find no charge or fault ... in him" (Dan. 6:4).

11. Is strong in faith — no matter what (I Tim. 6:12).

12. Is sensitive to the Holy Spirit's leading.

13. At times, takes risks.

14. Controls his/her personal finances — sets an example.

15. Has a grateful spirit (Col. 1:11,12).

16. Takes strong stand against evil.

17. Can shift gears without losing balance. Is able to change directions — discontinue programs that have served their time and purpose — change jobs, move. Paul wrote, "I have learned in whatever state I am, to be content" (Phil. 4:11).

18. Shows love for lost people, regardless of their background.

19. Is able to work well with others (Psa. 133). Daniel served under four kings.

20. Is not intimidated or threatened by people with greater talents in some areas than his/her own.

21. Surrounds himself/herself with prayerfully-selected, strong men or women. Works for unity.

22. Takes quality time with family and friends.

23. Is alert to God's times and seasons (Eccl. 3:1-8).

24. Rules his/her own spirit (Prov. 16:32).

25. Is self-disciplined, making best use of time. Selects priorities. "Seek the LORD and His strength; seek His

face evermore!" (I Chr. 16:11).

26. Must rule his/her own soul: will, emotion, mind. Every act starts with a choice for either good or evil.

27. Must rule his/her body: exercise, sleep, eat, work schedules — pacing oneself is necessary.

28. Must set the example by obeying God's command of paying tithes and giving offerings (Mal. 3:10-12). "For where your treasure is, there your heart will be also" (Matt. 6:21).

29. Must stay humble (Prov. 16:19; Tit. 3:2) and give all glory to God (I Cor. 3:7).

30. Must draw from the past, serve and be dedicated to the present, and have a consuming vision for the future. "Where *there is* no vision, the people perish: but he that keepth the law, happy *is* he" (Prov. 29:18 KJV).

31. Is chosen to rule a church as pastor, teacher — to make disciples, and to train world changers.

32. Must learn to rule well. Jesus said to one disciple, "Well *done*, good and faithful servant; you have been faithful over a few things, I will make you ruler over many things" (Matt. 25:23). "God *is* the Judge: He puts down one, and exalts another" (Psa. 75:7).

The buck stops with the leader. Dunn & Bradstreet said that 92 percent of annual business failures are due to management deficiencies. God needs successful godly business leaders — in every field.

One day, we'll help rule heaven and judge angels. "Do you not know that we shall judge angels? How much more, things that pertain to this life?" (I Cor. 6:3).

Chapter Thirty-Six

Prayer That Gets Results

Gordon used to say, "Make prayer a business in your life."

Prayer is talking to God.

I. How Do We Pray?

    A. Always go to the Father through Jesus.

    B. In confession and humility. Like Ezra (Ezra 10:1); and the publican (Lk. 18:13,14).

    C. Kinds of prayer.

        1. Soft, quiet prayer like Hannah — "Only her lips moved" (I Sam. 1:13).

        2. Violent prayer — "The kingdom of heaven suffers violence, and the violent take it by force" (Matt. 11:12).

            a. Gordon used to say, "Every man ought to pray at least one violent prayer each day."

            b. Isaiah prayed, "Oh, that You would rend the heavens!" (Isa. 64:1).

            c. Jesus — *"My God, My God, why have*

You forsaken Me?" (Matt. 27:46).

d. Elizabeth — "Spoke out with a loud voice" when she blessed Jesus (Lk.1:42).

3. Fervent prayer — "The effective, fervent prayer of a righteous man avails much" (Jas. 5:16).

4. Prayer of dominion — "Let them have dominion" (Gen. 1:26).

5. Pray in faith — "The prayer of faith will save the sick" (Jas. 5:15).

6. Pray alone — in your closet or room (Matt. 6:6).

7. Pray with husband, wife or prayer partner — one shall "chase a thousand, and two put ten thousand to flight" (Deut. 32:30).

8. Have a family altar daily — the family that prays together stays together.

9. Pray with hands raised — "Lift up your hands *in* the sanctuary" (Psa. 134:2).

10. Pray in unity (Acts 2:1,4; 4:24).

11. Pray with our understanding (I Cor. 14:15).

12. Pray with the Spirit (I Cor. 14:15).

a. You'll always pray in God's will.

b. It will be impossible to pray a selfish prayer.

c. You can pray about things of which you may know nothing.

13. Worshipful singing in one's language or in

the Spirit is one of the highest types of
prayer.

II.   Why Pray?

    A.   We have this confidence that God hears us. (I Jn.
5:14,15); "Oh God ... You who hear prayer"
(Psa. 65:1,2). "His ears *are open* to their cry"
(Psa. 34:15). (See also Psa. 34:17.)

    B.   Past personal experiences proved God answered
our prayers.

    C.   God has promised strength, guidance and
wisdom. "If any of you lacks wisdom, let him
ask of God" (Jas. 1:5).

III.   Pray When?

    A.   David prayed "Evening and morning and at
noon" (Psa. 55:17).

    B.   Daniel prayed, "With his windows open ... he
knelt down on his knees three times that day"
(Dan. 6:10); as Jim Goll titled his new book,
Kneeling on the Promises.

    C.   Paul recommended "Pray without ceasing"
(I Thes. 5:17).

    D.   Paul also urged "In everything by prayer"
(Phil. 4:6).

    E.   In trouble. "Call upon Me in the day of trouble;
I will deliver you" (Psa. 50:15).

    F.   To resist temptation. "Watch and pray, lest you
enter into temptation" (Matt. 26:41).

IV.   For Whom Do We Pray?

A.   Make a prayer list and carry it in your Bible.

B.   For your family — "Believe on the Lord Jesus Christ, and you will be saved, you and your household" (Acts 16:31). For what shall it profit men or women if they gain the whole world and lose their family?

C.   For rulers — "First of all ... for all men, for kings and all who are in authority" (I Tim. 2:1,2).

D.   For laborers — "Pray the Lord of the harvest to send out laborers" (Matt. 9:38).

E.   For one another (Jas. 5:14,16).

F.   For the sick and afflicted (Jas. 5:14,16).

G.   For your enemies — "Pray for those who spitefully use you" (Matt. 5:44).

H.   For protection — "The angel of the LORD encamps all around those who fear Him, and delivers them" (Psa. 34:7).

I.   For the peace of Jerusalem — "I will bless those who bless you (Israel), and I will curse him who curses you (Israel)" (Gen. 12:3 and Psa. 122:6).

V.   How Often Should We Pray?

A.   Daily for our needs — "Give us this day our daily bread" (Matt. 6:11).

B.   We can sin by ceasing to pray for certain individuals (I Sam. 12:23).

C.   We must "be instant in season, out of season" (II Tim. 4:2 KJV). Be ready at any time when the Spirit urges us.

D. It's up to us. David prayed, "I *give myself to* prayer" (Psa. 109:4).

E. Make prayer a business in your life. A businessman opens his shop daily, regularly. Set a time to do business with God. Jesus separated Himself and went aside to pray (Mk. 6:46; Lk. 6:12).

VI. The Wrong Way to Pray?

A. "Whatever *is* not from faith is sin" (Rom. 14:23). There is a difference between prayer and the prayer of faith.

B. "You shall not be like the hypocrites. … They love to pray … that they may be seen by men" (Matt. 6:5).

C. "Do not use vain repetitions as the heathen *do*" (Matt. 6:7).

VII. Fasting Breaks the Yoke.

A. Jonah fasted for Nineveh, Queen Esther to save the Jewish people, Moses, Daniel, Anna the prophetess, Paul with the crew aboard a sinking ship — all received miraculous answers.

B. Fasting should begin and end with praise — "Enter into His gates with thanksgiving, *and* into His courts with praise" (Psa. 100:4). "His praise *shall* continually *be* in my mouth" (Psa. 34:1). "Seven times a day I praise You, because of Your righteous judgments," said David (Psa. 119:164). David prayed three times daily (Psa. 55:17),and praised seven times each day!

VIII. Who Should Praise God?

    A.   "Let everything that has breath praise the LORD" (Psa. 150:6). The only excuse for not praising the Lord is being out of breath!

    B.   "Whoever offers praise glorifies Me" (Psa. 50:23). God in turn gives "a garment of praise for the spirit of heaviness" (Isa. 61:3). Put it on.

IX.   Why Don't All Congregations Praise the Lord?

    A.   The Bible says, "The living, the living man, he shall praise You" (Isa. 38:19) — a double emphasis.

    B.   "Death cannot praise You" (Isa. 38:18). "The dead do not praise the LORD" (Psa. 115:17).

    C.   The answer? Dead churches don't praise the Lord!

Chapter Thirty-Seven

How to be a Winner

Why should you endeavor to be a winner — to be on the cutting edge? So you can do more for God!

God has a plan for those who love Him: "I know the thoughts that I think toward you, says the LORD, thoughts of peace and not of evil, to give you a future and a hope" (Jer. 29:11).

Here are 10 principles all beginning with a "W" that will help you lay a solid foundation for your life — for your family, your business, your church.

I.   Word of God

    A.   Spend time daily in the Bible. Meditate on it; memorize it. (When I was in Bible school, I was challenged to read the Bible through each year. I accepted that challenge, and this year, I am reading my Bible through for the 64th time. [Three chapters daily and five on Sunday will do it.] The Word has kept me going for God!)

    B.   God has tremendous blessings in store for those who obey His Word. This is what He promised Israel, and these blessings are still available to the obedient: "It shall come to pass, if you diligently obey the voice of the LORD your God, to observe carefully all His commandments which I command you today, that the LORD your God will set you high above all nations of the earth. And all these blessings shall come upon you and overtake you, because you obey the voice of the LORD your God" (Deut. 28:1,2). The Lord goes on to list the blessings of following Him (Deut 28: 3-14).

C. There are also curses for disobedience (Deut. 28:15-68). So it's important that you have your priorities straight. And knowing God and His Word should be at the top of your list.

D. God wants His Word in our hearts and our minds: "And these words which I command you today shall be in your heart. You shall teach them diligently to your children, and shall talk of them when you sit in your house, when you walk by the way, when you lie down, and when you rise up" (Deut. 6:6,7).

E. The Old Testament blessings (and curses) apply to those who trust in Christ. Paul said that we must believe, "just as Abraham *'believed God, and it was accounted to him for righteousness.'* Therefore know that *only* those who are of faith are sons of Abraham. And the Scripture, foreseeing that God would justify the Gentiles by faith, preached the gospel to Abraham beforehand, saying, *'In you all the nations shall*

> *be blessed.'* So then those who *are* of faith are blessed with believing Abraham" (Gal. 3:6-9).

F.   The Bible tells us that Christ brought us an even better covenant than Abraham's. The prophet Jeremiah foretold it (Jer. 31:31-34), and the writer of Hebrews expounds on it (Heb. 8:7-13). You will only discover the benefits of the new covenant as you study the Word of God.

II.   Worship

A.   *Webster's Dictionary* says that worship is "to regard with **great**, even **extravagant** respect, honor, or devotion."

B.   God wants our prayer, our petitions, our supplication. But remember, even atheists petition God when they're desperate.

C.   God wants our confession — our acknowledgement of our sin.

D.   God wants our praise and adoration; they express our regard for Him.

E.   God wants our gratefulness — our expression of appreciation for the many blessings He bestows upon us.

F.   But He wants more than these: He desires our worship. Worship is loving Him just for Who He is. It's the highest form of communication with Him. Worship should be reserved for God alone; He is a jealous God (Ex. 34:14).

III.   Warfare

A.   There are two things a Christian needs to know:

1. What the devil can do to you.

   a. Satan will try to sidetrack you so you will lose your effectiveness as a witness.

   b. Satan will try to accuse you (Job 1:12; (Zech. 3:1,2).

   c. Satan has evil schemes (II Cor. 2:11).

   d. Anger gives the devil a foothold (Eph. 4:27).

   e. Satan is the tempter (Matt. 4:1-11; I Thes. 3:5).

2. What you can do to the devil.

   a. Don't try to negotiate with him. Use spiritual weapons: "Though we walk in the flesh, we do not war according to the flesh. For the weapons of our warfare *are* not carnal but mighty in God for pulling down strongholds" (II Cor. 10:3,4).

      • Prayer (Eph. 6:17,18)

      • The Word (Heb. 4:12)

      • Fasting

      • Praise

      • Worship

   b. God protects His children from the devil (I Jn. 5:18).

B. Keep your balance.

   1. Don't ride a hobbyhorse or get off on a tangent.

IV. Wisdom

    A. Wisdom is the proper use of knowledge. It is not only having knowledge and understanding of people and situations, but the discernment and good judgment needed to deal with them.

    B. Solomon was known as the wisest man of his day. When God asked him what he desired, he responded, "Give to Your servant an understanding heart to judge Your people, that I may discern between good and evil" (I Ki. 3:9).

        1. "Happy *is* the man *who* finds wisdom" (Prov. 3:13).

        2. "The fear of the LORD *is* the beginning of wisdom" (Prov. 9:10).

    C. Jesus spoke of the importance of wisdom:

        1. "Be wise as serpents and harmless as doves" (Matt. 10:16).

        2. Jesus promised that when we are persecuted for His sake, "I will give you a mouth and wisdom which all your adversaries will not be able to contradict or resist" (Lk. 21:15).

    D. James encouraged, "If any of you lacks wisdom, let him ask of God" (Jas. 1:5).

    E. Wisdom is needed in the family:

        1. "Through wisdom a house is built, and by understanding it is established" (Prov. 24:3).

        2. It is said, "The family that prays together, stays together." That is true. Also true: "The

family that plays together, stays together."

V. Weight

   A. It's important to take care of the body; it's the temple of the Holy Spirit (I Cor. 3:16,17).

      1. We are "fearfully *and* wonderfully made" (Psa. 139:14).

   B. We should not abuse our bodies.

      1. Gluttony, voracious eating and drinking, is condemned (Prov. 23:21).

         a. Paul speaks of those whose god is their appetite (Phil. 3:19).

         b. David Wilkerson: "Never in all my life, as I've traveled over the world, have I seen so many Christians so much overweight as in the U.S."

         c. Some are overweight simply because they are not careful about the kinds of food and the portions they eat. A very few are overweight because of health problems. With most, it's an addiction that can be overcome with God's help.

      2. Drunkenness is condemned.

         a. "Wine *is* a mocker, strong drink *is* a brawler, and whoever is led astray by it is not wise" (Prov. 20:1).

      3. Jesus refused drugs, even when He was dying an excruciatingly painful death (Matt. 27:34).

   4. Smoking is injurious to one's body — the temple of the Holy Spirit (I. Cor. 3:16,17).

VI. Witness

 A. Christians are to be witnesses everywhere they go.

   1. "You shall receive power when the Holy Spirit has come upon you; and you shall be witnesses to Me in Jerusalem, and in all Judea and Samaria, and to the end of the earth" (Acts 1:8).

   2. To Philemon, Paul wrote that he had heard of his love and faith in the Lord and all the saints. He prayed "that the sharing of your faith may become effective by the acknowledgment of every good thing which is in you in Christ Jesus" (Phi. 6).

   3. Stan Cottrell is a modern-day example of a witness. He is a marathon runner, and ran the China Wall. One of the top Chinese officials asked him, "What makes America such a great nation?" Stan pulled a coin out of his pocket and asked the communist to read it: "In God We Trust." Stan said, "That's on all our coins and currency. As long as we obey that, we'll be great."

VII. Work

 A. We must follow Jesus' example: "I must work the works of Him who sent Me while it is day; *the* night is coming when no one can work"

(Jn. 9:4).

1. How you use your time, including your leisure hours, determines how successful you are.

B. Faith without works is dead (Jas. 2:14-18).

1. Ministry is a four-letter word spelled "W-O-R-K."

VIII. Wealth

A. Obedience to God's principles brings God's blessing, including wealth (Deut. 8:7-20).

1. In many nations, owning a pair of shoes means wealth.

2. Proving God's faithfulness in rewarding obedience by tithing will release God's blessing (Mal. 3:8-16).

B. The "rich" are to share their wealth.

1. "Command those who are rich in this present age not to be haughty, nor to trust in uncertain riches but in the living God, who gives us richly all things to enjoy. *Let them* do good, that they be rich in good works, ready to give, willing to share" (I Tim. 6:17,18).

a. Plant your best seed in a ministry that is producing.

2. God is debtor to no man: "He who has pity on the poor lends to the LORD, and He will pay back what he has given" (Prov. 19:17).

3.   Those who are generous will be blessed (Prov. 22:9).

4.   "Give to him who asks you, and from him who wants to borrow from you do not turn away" (Matt. 5:42).

5.   What a phenomenal rewards system God has! "Give, and it will be given to you: good measure, pressed down, shaken together, and running over will be put into your bosom. For with the same measure that you use, it will be measured back to you" (Lk. 6:38). Hang on to it, and you'll lose it.

IX.   Winner's Attitude

A.   Paul said, "I can do all things through Christ who strengthens me" (Phil. 4:13).

1.   With God's help, we can do a lot of things we're not qualified to do. Our hindrances: negative mindset, suspicion, skepticism, fear, jealousy, criticism.

B.   David said, "The LORD *is* on my side; I will not fear. What can man do unto me?" (Psa. 118:6).

X.   World Vision

A.   "Go into all the world" (Mk. 16:15).

1.   About 250 international students attend our Dallas Bible-training center, Christ For The Nations Institute, each year. In our 29 years of training world changers, we've had few dropouts among the internationals. Over

26,000 students — from every state in the Union and more than 100 nations — have attended CFNI. Now we have 40 associated Bible schools in 29 countries. We have helped build nearly 10,400 Native Churches, supplied millions of free Christian books and Bibles, helped several orphanages, and sent many tons of food, clothing and medical supplies to needy nations.

B. "Lift up your eyes and look at the fields, for they are already white to harvest!" (Jn. 4:35).

Conclusion

A s we move into the next century, unknown to man but not to God, our faith is in Him! As I was thinking on some of the dire predictions, by believers and non-believers as well, I wondered if the Lord still has the recipe for manna, and concluded He does!

Here at Christ For The Nations' headquarters, Dennis, my youngest son, who became president when I stepped down in 1985, has selected a team of CFNI alumni, anointed and ready to carry on the vision, to continue to reach the world with the Gospel. Among them are Randy Bozarth, vice president, and Dr. Larry Hill, executive director of CFNI, both of whom, with their wives, graduated in the 70s; also Mark Ott, business affairs director, with his assistant, Tom Tuning, and Dr. Harold Reents, academic dean. The director of our new program in Spanish — Instituto Bíblico en Español — Palemón Camu, is also an alumnus. Plus many others in key positions on our full-time staff are graduates, including directors of a number of our overseas Bible schools, and pastors of many of our Native Churches.

So with our "generation following" team, handpicked by God, and trained to be world changers, I see them now as they are getting their "second wind," racing toward the finish line — the generation, I believe, that will see the return of

Jesus to establish His Kingdom — the new heavens and the new earth!

The Lord's directive to all is: "Watch and pray" (Matt. 26:41).

SPECIAL NOTE: A free gift subscription to CHRIST FOR THE NATIONS magazine is available to those who write to Christ For The Nations, P.O. Box 769000, Dallas, TX 75376-9000. This magazine contains special feature stories of men of faith and includes prophetic articles on the latest world developments. Why not include the names of your friends? (Due to high mailing rates, this applies only to Canada and the U.S.)

FREDA LINDSAY —
A woman who believes faith is practical!

In **My Diary Secrets,** Freda recounts her courtship and marriage to Gordon Lindsay and their life of ministry. Together they founded Christ For The Nations, a missionary organization that reaches around the world, and its interdenominational Bible institute, which has trained more than 26,000. This is an unforgettable story of God's anointing on a couple who devoted their lives to His service.

$9.95

In **Freda: The Widow Who Took Up the Mantle,** Mrs. Lindsay continues her life's chronicle, sharing how God enabled her to carry on the ministry He had given them after Gordon's death.

$4.95

$7.95

A Book of Miracles relates how God's promised provision has been faithfully provided throughout her lifetime.

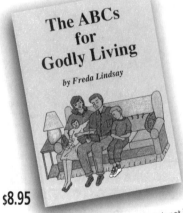

$8.95

The ABCs for Godly Living is not just for children — parents and grandparents will benefit, too, from its words of wisdom. It covers salvation, healing, love, discipline, the Holy Spirit and many other subjects.

$25

Christ For The Nations: The Golden Jubilee traces the history of Christ For The Nations from its inception as *The Voice of Healing* magazine in 1948 to its present state as a multifaceted ministry with a vision for global evangelization.

Please add $2 per book for postage and handling.

CFN Books • P.O. Box 769000 • Dallas, TX 75376-9000
(214) 302-6276